Don't Die in the Bush

By the same authors

Sven Klinge
CLASSIC WALKS OF AUSTRALIA
AUSTRALIAN MOUNTAINS: The Best 100 Walks
(with Tyrone T Thomas)
CYCLING THE BUSH: 100 Rides in New South Wales
CYCLING THE BUSH: 100 Rides in Victoria
CYCLING THE BUSH: 100 Rides in Tasmania
CYCLING THE BUSH: The Best Rides in Australia
MOUNTAIN BIKING: The Fundamentals

Adrian Hart
SHORT SHRIFTS: Confessions of a High School Heretic

Visit Sven Klinge's *Wilderness Australia* web page at www.zeta.org.au/~avatar.
Sven can be emailed at avatar@zeta.org.au
Visit Adrian Hart's web page at www.zeta.org.au/~ady.
Adrian can be emailed at ady@zeta.org.au

Don't Die in the Bush

The Complete Guide to Australian Camping

Sven Klinge and Adrian Hart

NEW
HOLLAND

First published in Australia in 2000 by
New Holland Publishers (Australia) Pty Ltd
Sydney • Auckland • London • Cape Town

14 Aquatic Drive Frenchs Forest NSW 2086 Australia
218 Lake Road Northcote Auckland New Zealand
24 Nutford Place London W1H 6DQ United Kingdom
80 McKenzie Street Cape Town 8001 South Africa

National Library of Australia Cataloguing-in-publication data:

Klinge, Sven, 1969–
   Don't die in the bush: the complete guide to Australian camping.

   Bibliography.
   Includes Index
   ISBN 1 86436 525 0

   1. Camping – Australia – Handbooks, manuals, etc.
   2. Camping – Australia – Equipment and supplies.
   1. Hart, Adrian, 1971–. Title.

   796.54

Publishing Manager: Anouska Good
Project Coordinator: Sean Doyle
Copy Editor: Glenda Downing
Designer: Andrew Cunningham, Studio Pazzo
Cover Design: Peta Nugent
Printer: Times Offset, Malaysia.

Please note: While all care has been taken to ensure the information
contained in this book is correct at time of publication, the authors and publisher
accept no liability for any accident, injury, or other misadventure incurred by
relying on the advice in this book.

About the authors

Sven Klinge began venturing into the Australian wilderness in 1987, exploring a host of national parks and state forests on foot and mountain bike. He wrote his first book, *Cycling The Bush: 100 Rides in New South Wales*, a year later, aged nineteen. The *Cycling the Bush* series, including *The Best Rides in Australia*, comprises Australia's premier mountain biking guidebooks. Sven's landscape photography has also been featured in various guidebooks, advertisements and magazine articles. Sven has also co-authored a major national walking title on Australia's mountains with Tyrone Thomas. *Classic Walks of Australia* is his next project.

While Sven has toured extensively throughout Australia, New Zealand and Europe, it is the great mountain wilderness World Heritage Areas of south-west Tasmania and Fiordland that particularly draw his attention.

Educated at Sydney University, Sven currently works as an accountant, contract network administrator, and freelance writer for legal journals.

Adrian Hart has travelled extensively throughout Australia, New Zealand, North America and Europe. He has walked, camped and cycled in many of Australia's national parks. His interest in the outdoors now pushes him to new challenges in extreme sports, which he is researching for a new Australian reference guide.

Adrian graduated from Sydney University, where he now works as an Associate Lecturer. Adrian has worked as a research assistant, college tutor, information research officer and volunteer news reporter for public radio station 2SER-FM. In 1996, he published his first novel, *Short Shrifts: Confessions of a High School Heretic*. Adrian divides his time between Sydney and Bundanoon, where he pursues an interest in photography, astronomy and outdoor sports.

Kookaburra

Contents

Acknowledgments

Much appreciation goes to the following people, companies and organisations for their support in the publication of this guidebook: Anouska Good at New Holland Publishers; Fraser McLachlan and Katherine McRoberts at Macpac Wilderness Equipment; Andrew Hanna at the Land Information Centre, New South Wales (topographical maps); David Moss at Mountain Designs (camping equipment); Ian Gibson at Paddy Pallin (camping equipment); Grant Minervini and Guy Reynolds at Cascade Designs (camping accessories); Tim Campbell at Adventure Designs/One Planet/Aiking (camping equipment); David Huxley at Berrivale Orchards (Isosport isotonic sports drinks); Paul Gibbs at Maxwell (Lowepro photographic camera bags); Sarah Moulder at Kathmandu (camping equipment); Greg Foord at Spelean (Sweetwater Guardian water purifiers); Tracey Orr at AUSLIG, Canberra (topographical AUSMAPs); Robert Avery at TASMAP (topographical maps); D. Nicholls, M. Enjeti and B. Johnston at the Tasmanian Department of Tourism; Adrian Goodrich at the Department of Natural Resources and Environment, Victoria; John Lane at the South Australian Department of Environment and Natural Resources; Graham Stanton at the Queensland Department of Natural Resources (topographical maps); Martin Hanley at Hanley Trading (outdoor accessories); Noel McFarlane at Bunyip Bags (panniers); Tom Andrews at Macson Trading Company (Avocet Vertech altimeter); Fuji (film); Salomon (hiking boots); and Tyrone T. Thomas, Lara Connor and Emma L. Vedris.

Preface

This book updates many of the obsolete camping practices of the last few decades, incorporating the contemporary eco-sensitive approach that helps minimise the impact of ever-increasing numbers of campers on our environment. In addition, many of the very latest advances in technology have been incorporated—what the acronyms mean, how they work, and what features to watch out for when purchasing. We've tried to write in an informative, yet entertaining manner, hoping to eliminate much of the blatantly obvious commonsense advice that fills other books, such as 'don't pick up snakes', 'don't panic in an emergency', etc.

Each section deals with specific issues related to camping, and unlike other books, is specifically targeted towards Australians, novices and hardened veterans alike. Finally, the last section looks ahead to the future and speculates how camping will evolve further in the next few decades.

Satinash eucalypt

Introduction:
Australians and the bush

Modern Australia is still searching for the ideal balance between development and environmental preservation. Whereas in the past taming the environment was seen as a laudable human achievement, today almost the opposite is true. Now the ability to live with the environment, and not against it, is becoming the prevailing wisdom. In a sense, attitudes towards the bush are turning full circle. The customs and beliefs of Australia's Aboriginal peoples are receiving greater emphasis; there is a growing recognition of the symbiotic relationship they forged with the land.

Combining a natural love for the outdoor life with environmental passion and a sense of adventure, more and more Australians are heading out into the bush to camp, walk, canoe, climb and explore. As we enter the twenty-first century, camping technology is big business. With space-age materials such as Gore-Tex, kevlar, and titanium helping to produce lighter, smaller and stronger gear, outdoor enthusiasts can have complete confidence when venturing into the wildest terrain.

The bush is a place of scenic wonder, an ecological ark, a safe haven from the troubles and stress of modern living, a vacation retreat, a physical challenge, a store of genetic diversity, an icon for environmental values. It is ingrained in our history, art and culture. It is an intrinsic part of us.

Mottelecah eucalypt

Equipment: For tech-heads and gadget-freaks

Camping equipment was initially very primitive. Early walkers used kerosene cans, bags tied to poles, and sugar sacks to store gear, others even used wheelbarrows. Photographs taken before the First World War reveal walkers carrying shearer's swags. These were later modified to 'dungal' swags, which were balanced for walking by having two halves: one bag would rest against the chest and the other against the back. The two parts were attached by fabric that lay across one shoulder. Myles Dunphy, one of the most famous early pioneers, whose name later became synonymous with the conservation movement, experimented with the design and loading of these swags. He also helped design a tent, which was made from white calico with eaves through which a cotton rope could slide. If poles for the frame and pegs to secure the guy ropes were needed, they were cut from the surrounding scrub at each campsite, as were fern fronds and bark for softer, raised bedding. There were no tent zippers, so the occupants had to contend with mosquitoes and bugs.

Unfortunately, the calico wasn't waterproof, and campers looked to other fabrics that might suit their requirements. They found the cloth used in sails was ideal as it was light, compressible and kept out the elements. Called japara, it's a tightly woven Egyptian cotton fabric that soon became used for packs, rain-capes (which doubled as groundsheets), and sleeping bag liners.

By the time of the Second World War, packs were made of canvas with an A-frame and had leather straps. They cost around $10.00 at the time, and weighed about 2.5 kilograms. They were the first materials to combine breathability with waterproofness. By the 1950s, nylon entered the market.

Hobnailed boots were the standard footwear before more comfortable sneakers became available. Paddy Pallin was the first person to start manufacturing quality durable specific-bushwalking/camping equipment in Australia and he sold his own designs from a shop in George Street near Wynyard station. Today the franchise is renowned throughout Australia, more than 70 years since its inception.

* * *

While weather and terrain can conspire against them, campers can have control over one element—the gear they take along. The use of appropriate equipment can make the difference between a pleasant, exciting adventure with all the luxury items included, and an arduous feat of endurance taking along nothing more than a compass, foam mat and a sense of the impossible. Camping has enjoyed a boom in technology and fabrics, which all add to comfort, reliability and safety.

Clothing

Waterproof jackets

Mountains attract violent weather changes because of the sudden height variation. The nature of the topography can obscure storm fronts until they're almost overhead. This necessitates wearing an outer-shell garment that is windproof, waterproof, breathable, lightweight and compactable.

Ever since its introduction in the late 1970s, the de facto standard in outdoor jacket material worldwide has been Gore-Tex, which satisfies all the above requirements. This impressive fabric is manufactured from a semi-permeable, microporous membrane that allows the skin to breathe (that is, the sweat is allowed to evaporate) while simultaneously preventing any external moisture from entering. Gore-Tex fabrics are windproof to a specification of less than one cubic foot per minute. This means total wind protection in wind velocities over 33 km/h, which helps to prevent heat loss and is thus extremely handy in the outdoors in a variety of conditions.

Mountain Designs carries a range of Gore-Tex jackets, such as the cirro-stratus. It is knee-length and contains a variety of pockets for maps, wallet and food. For even harsher climates, Paddy Pallin sells the Vortex full-zip overpants, which gives the legs the same protection from the elements as the jacket gives the torso. They are made from Ripstop and three-layer Gore-Tex, and are moderately expensive.

Fleece jackets

The primary disadvantage of Gore-Tex is that while it may help keep you relatively dry, it won't keep you warm. In cold alpine climates, one needs a warmer jacket to go under the Gore-Tex shell. Gore Windstopper or Polartec Windbloc fleece jackets are breathable, windproof, warm and moisture resistant. Polartec fleece is designed to trap air and to be used as the insulating medium in an item of clothing. Its features include high breathability and durability. The open nature of the pile allows body vapour to pass through the fabric and the fibres do not absorb water. The pile finish on both sides of the fleece provides a large surface area that can withstand punishment over many seasons. The pile doesn't separate, the fabric will not stretch out of shape, and it is colour fast. Conveniently, it has also been treated to resist mildew.

Underwear

Moisture-wicking polypropylene or Polartec thermal underwear is the most effective material for insulation next to the skin. These garments, available from Kathmandu, are extremely efficient in their warmth retention despite their compact size and light weight.

Thermal clothes

Extreme conditions will necessitate the use of a set of thermal insulation waterproof gloves and socks. Sealskinz socks are insulated by thermax and contain a waterproofing membrane from Du-Pont that is perfect for high-rainfall muddy areas such as south-west Tasmania and Fiordland. When dressing for warmth, a three-layer approach is optimal and flexible. This comprises an inner thermal layer of underwear that keeps the skin dry, a breathable fleece layer for maximum warmth retention, and an outer Gore-Tex waterproof shell to keep out wind and rain.

Boots

Hiking boots have evolved considerably over the years since their military origins. They have been adapted to be waterproof, softer and more comfortable. When purchasing boots, look for the following features:

- lightweight (not much more than one kilogram) to reduce energy consumption
- waterproof: quality boots have a membrane between the inner and outer layers
- tread: good grip for traversing rocks and mossy boulders
- size: make sure they fit well with a pair of thick socks
- accessories: will the boot work with a gaiter?

Packs

Daypack

The walker's main luggage carrier will be a daypack, preferably one that's divided up into three or more compartments. It should be comfortable, have a waist strap, and enough room for plenty of water, food, maps and a camera.

Macpac manufactures an excellent range of small packs, such as the 35-litre Ultramarathon. Besides having a comfortable and comprehensive harness, it also can fit the optional Macpac Oasis water bladder. This 3.2-litre collapsible carrier can be inserted into a sleeve in the daypack, and a hose then attached onto the shoulder strap for easy access to fluids without having to take off the pack.

One Planet also manufactures an overnight pack (the Bass) in 65-and 75-litre models that has a detachable 26-litre daypack, allowing for an extremely high degree of flexibility.

Water bladders

Also known as 'camel backs' or 'hydration packs', these popular accessories address the need for walkers to constantly rehydrate themselves. They come in various sizes and have the advantage of being lightweight and easy to use. An example is the 6-litre One Planet H2O pack which can be used on its own or attached to other One Planet backpacks. A hose from the clear plastic bladder in the pack can be attached on the front harness to allow on-the-go drinking. One word of warning: don't use powdered flavours in the water on hot days unless the bladder is flushed out immediately because bacteria can accumulate from the sugar residue. The longest use will come from filling them only with clear purified water. Keep the bladder refrigerated before each camp.

Special-use packs

Campers sometimes wish to carry special gear along, such as photographic equipment. In panniers, expensive cameras would only get damaged with the constant vibration. Lowepro makes a series of specific photographic backpacks, such as the Photo Trekker AW, which comes with its own protective waterproof in case of rain. The pack can house 35 mm SLR and medium-format cameras, with separate compartments for lenses, filters, film and other accessories.

On some day trips, a normal 20–30 litre daypack is insufficient to carry a change of warm weather gear and other accessories. That's why a medium-sized pack, like the Macpac Rocketeer or One Planet Mistress can be very handy. They're just as strong as a heavy-duty overnight pack, but without the additional weight. They can hold around 40–50 litres in several versatile compartments.

Pack towels

A very useful multipurpose 68 x 25 centimetre cloth made from 100 per cent viscose can hold up to ten times its weight in water. This water can be 92 per cent wrung out by hand, and the remainder quickly dries when exposed to air. Weighing just 42 grams, it's the ideal towel for the hard-core camper. Use it to dry the skin, as insulation for hot pots, cleaning the dishes, a neckerchief for sweat absorption, or a medical compress.

Navigational aids

Altimeter

An altimeter can be of great assistance with navigational queries by reconciling altitude with topographical information on maps to help locate your position.

Compass

The humble compass is the most fundamental navigation device. The majority of compasses sold in camping stores are standardised. For a more detailed description of using compasses, see pages 29–34.

Global Positioning System (GPS)

A GPS unit can best be described as a foolproof electronic compass, presenting readings for altitude, exact longitude and latitude as well as a host of other useful navigational data, including direction travelled, average speed and estimated time of arrival at destination. Recent advances in technology have reduced the weight and size of GPS units to become comparable with mobile phones. The GPS uses 24 (soon to be 30) navigation satellite communications orbiting the earth every 12 hours at 20 000 kilometres to locate a receiver's position on the planet. Initially developed to guide ballistic missiles to their targets, civilian users of this 'free' global service now predominate.

Each of the satellites carries four atomic clocks that are so accurate that they vary only three seconds every million years. The exact position of each satellite over the earth can be precisely predicted mathematically at any given time because its orbit follows the measurable laws of relativity and gravitation.

GPS positioning errors

The US Department of Defense varies the satellite signals to insert errors which degrade their accuracy. This apparently reduces the risk of an enemy camper using GPS to steer missiles aimed at the United States. The accuracy restriction, known as Selective Availability (SA), results in horizontal position errors of less than 100 metres 95 per cent of the time.

For a hiker in forested areas, leaves can weaken the signals. Moving a few feet or simply continuing walking may improve the signal strengths. In clear areas, reception of eight satellites is relatively easy. Therefore it is important to ask for a 12-channel receiver when you purchase a GPS unit.

Overnight gear

After some preliminary car camps in the nearest national park, overnight walking might be the next step undertaken. The times immediately before, during and after sunset give nature an ambience that day visitors miss out on. The trees' silver leaves glow a brilliant red, the wind stops and the only sound audible is the crackling of logs in the campfire. As with day-trip equipment, only essential gear should be purchased at first.

Overnight backpack

The crucial factors to consider when choosing a quality brand name backpack are:

- harness: is it comfortable and can it be shaped to your torso?
- material: is it tough and waterproof?
- compartments: can your gear be divided up for ease of access?
- zippers: are they strong enough to last several years?

Make sure the harness is fully adjustable so that the weight is distributed evenly between your shoulders and hips. Although external compartment packs are rare these days, most good packs now have several internal compartments for dividing up gear. The pack should be waterproof, and accommodate enough equipment for at least a week.

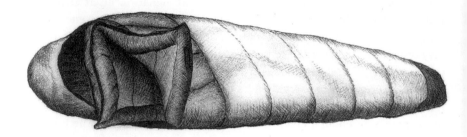

Sleeping bag

These vary in price enormously. Supermarkets sell very cheap polyester bags that weigh 2–3 kilograms, adequate for summer camping in relatively warm climates or by the coast. Slightly more upmarket are synthetic Quallofill bags that are relatively warm even when wet. The disadvantage is that they're very bulky.

It is difficult to go past a fill comprising mainly duck or goose down. Imported from China, down is by far the best insulator because of its air-trapping qualities. Furthermore, down bags are light (1–2 kilograms) and can compress to incredibly small sizes. They range in price depending on the amount and ratio of the fill. The top models have waterproof Gore-Tex exteriors but they're unnecessary unless you are planning to camp in Antarctica or underwater.

Accessories also exist for sleeping bags:

- large storage bags, as down should not be compressed when not in use
- silk and cotton inner sheets to be added for extra warmth
- a full Gore-Tex bivvy outer lining (available at Paddy Pallin) that completely waterproofs the sleeping bag, reducing the need for a tent. Although costing $500, the bivvy compacts to a minute size and weighs less than a kilogram, which the back muscles will appreciate for many years to come.

Sleeping mat

Foam closed-cell sleeping rolls are recommended—unbeatable for their price. Supermarkets sell them for about $20, although some can cost up to $65. In cold or damp conditions, the ground will drain heat away during the night because the sleeping bag filler directly underneath will be

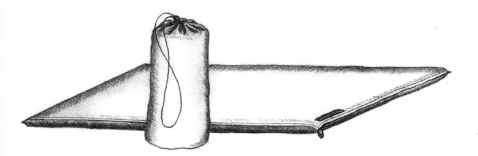

compressed. Proper insulation can be provided only with self-inflating foam mattresses, which are smaller than their closed-cell counterparts. They provide a cushion of air that shields the body from the ground. The disadvantage is that they can puncture. There are various manufacturers of these, but the Therma-A-Rest models from Cascade Designs are considered to be the strongest.

Tent

If you are camping on a clear summer night by Ningaloo Reef, a simple fly will keep the dew off. However, when venturing into uncertain territory, such as Port Davey, where sudden violent weather changes are unpredictable, a sealed tent is highly recommended. If camping in a group, the weight of the tent can be shared. The application of a seam-sealant and the use of a group sheet, preferably a space blanket, can improve water resistance. The design of the tent, where it's used, and how, will critically affect the comfort and feeling of security. Following is a description of the many factors that comprise the design.

Condensation

The average adult exhales about one litre of water overnight. This is in addition to any perspiration that may come from overheating the body. Using a stove inside a tent will also produce plenty of water vapour (as a by-product of burning fuel and also from the cooking pot).

Water vapour that can't escape from the confines of the tent will condense as droplets within the tent, primarily on cold surfaces, should the air temperature fall below the dew point. The result is damp and even sodden (and certainly heavier) sleeping bags, clothing and gear. So it's important to use a lightweight, breathable fabric as your inner wall.

Loss of warmth

At night, heat radiates from a tent skin, quickly lowering its temperature and the temperature of the air in contact with it. Humid air in the tent condenses on the inside surface of the tent fabric. Simultaneously, dew can fall on the outside. On cold nights when the temperature drops well below freezing, liquid condensation is bypassed and ice crystals form directly from moisture in the air. For these reasons, high alpine and polar tents sometimes feature a removable lining from which frost can be shaken.

Ventilation

Ventilation is crucial in keeping the inside of the tent dry and the key to minimising condensation. Unzipping the outer fly whenever possible, so air can circulate through the tent, facilitates ventilation.

Configuration

The single most important factor in a tent's ability to keep out the elements is the gap between the inner tent and the fly. The greater the gap, the less leeway there is for moisture to permeate from one surface to another.

Many modern tents, such as those from Eureka, Macpac and Wilderness Equipment, can be pitched so that the fly and tent are erected together. This is a big advantage in the rain, as the inner will hardly get wet. In some tents, the frame can either be fed into sleeves on the inner tent or just the outer fly, allowing flexibility in erection, depending on the type of conditions you expect to encounter.

Features

Seam sealing: The most essential function of a tent is to keep out the rain. Just like Gore-Tex jackets, it is crucial that all seams be factory tape-sealed.

Tent fabric: Nylon is the most commonly used fabric, as it is highly air-permeable, water-repellent, mildew-resistant and dries easily. Furthermore, nylon has a far better ability to absorb the shock loads of violent wind gusts.

Zips: High-quality YKK nylon coil zips with heavy-duty sliders should be fitted throughout the outer and inner tents. Most campers will find that zippers are often the first item to wear out on a tent, and hence the first that needs replacing. There are very few camping experiences more humiliating than having to share an expensive four-season tent with mosquitoes, flies and other bugs.

Tent floor: Quality tent floors are tub-designed. This means there are no ground edge seams or even corner seams, which considerably enhances waterproofing.

Frame: Most poles on three- and four-season tents today are manufactured from high-tensile, pre-curved, thin-walled aircraft aluminium alloy tubing. This tubing specification has been proven to possess the best combination of mechanical properties for lightweight tent structures. The shock-corded poles should be divided into sections no longer than the height of your backpack (usually about 75 centimetres). If the

design of the tent requires uneven-length poles, it is a good idea to colour-code the odd one out for ease of identification when pitching. There can be times when the light is fading, or when it's raining, when time is at a premium. Also check with the retailer that replacement poles are available in case one snaps.

Accessories

- **Separate storage compartments.** The weight of a tent is normally shared between party members, so separate bags allow the fly, inner, frame and pegs to be divided up.
- **Pegs.** If you don't own a self-supporting tent, try to buy a tent that comes with broad, aluminium, angled pegs. These provide the sturdiest support, and should be purchased separately if your tent doesn't contain them. Pegs might even be helpful on a self-supporting tent in severe winds.
- **Valances** are an advantage against snow spindrift, for securing tents in extreme winds, and for camping in extreme conditions. Although they can hinder ventilation, valances add to the stability of the tent. Brands such as Wilderness Equipment can be fitted after purchase or, if not required, can be removed without damage to the tent.
- **Repair kit.** Some manufacturers either supply a tent repair kit separately or include it with the tent. A repair kit typically contains spare fabric to sew over holes, seam-sealant for when the tent's factory sealant wears off and a temporary sleeve housing in the event of a pole snapping. The two broken poles can slot into a sleeve.

Recent tent designs employ new lightweight materials and technology. The classic new-age tent is the self-supporting dome. Gone are the days of carrying heavy steel frames, canvas, plastic ground floors, pegs, ropes and so on. No more drilling in hard surfaces and tripping over ropes. The self-supporting dome tent needs no pegs and no ropes. It is lightweight, has excellent space-to-weight ratio, good headroom, stability, ease and speed of erection, the ability to pitch on rock, as well as the fact that once set up it can simply be picked up and placed elsewhere. The only disadvantage with these self-supporting tents is that they can be blown away when no one is in them, so it's advisable to throw in all the sleeping gear and maybe a backpack immediately.

One such tent is the two-person Apollo from Macpac's Horizon series. While the tent itself is self-supporting, the fly needs only a minimum of two pegs to be secured.

The tunnel-style tent (sometimes crossbred with the dome, forming a 'dunnel' is also popular. It incorporates vestibules, is very light and is suitable for exposed high-altitude conditions. These are what the professional mountaineers use.

Groundsheet

The common space blanket can be bought at disposable stores everywhere and is by far the most popular groundsheet. Its uses include:

- a floor when using only a fly so sleeping bags don't get dirty
- an extra floor for a tent to help prevent heat escaping and water leaking in
- a picnic blanket
- an emergency blanket for victims of hypothermia and heat exhaustion.

With the silver side out, the blanket will reflect some 70 per cent of external radiation, keeping the body cool. The dark side is placed outside in the event of hypothermia, thus absorbing external radiation and reflecting internal radiation.

Tawny frogmouth

Basic Camping Techniques: A city-slicker's survival guide to beyond the outer suburbs

To enjoy Australia's national parks in comfort and safety, some basic skills and knowledge need to be developed. Fundamental bush and camp 'crafts' are easy to learn, being a mixture of common and uncommon sense: the former is instinctive and comes from within, while the latter is sourced from the stored knowledge and experiences of bushwalkers, campers and other outdoor enthusiasts over the generations. Once these basic skills have been learned, they open up a whole new world, allowing free exploration and adventure into some of the most spectacular scenery and natural beauty in Australia and overseas. This chapter presents some of the most intrinsic skills required for spending a day or two in the bush with friends—how to plan and prepare properly a wilderness trip, locate a good campsite and organise it for comfort, safety and environmental sensitivity. More advanced wilderness and survival skills will be discussed in the following chapter.

Preparation

While some of the best outdoor experiences seem to happen by luck and fate—a chance encounter with a kangaroo and joey along a remote mountain track, for instance—the likelihood of having such experiences at all can be increased remarkably through sound planning and preparation.

15

Sensible plans cannot only help reduce risks and dangers but also, by getting some of the little things right at the start, greatly enhance the fun of the whole outdoors experience. So, before setting out it is a good idea to have the following bases covered:

- establish the 'aim' of the trip
- organise the party size and who to take
- plan the camp destination/s and the route/s to get there
- make a food and equipment checklist and stick to it
- have some experience at pitching tents and lighting stoves and fires
- know some first aid techniques (see Chapter Five)
- know some basic bushcraft skills, such as map navigation
- inform family and friends of your plans.

The first point, the aim of the trip, may be as simple as hanging out by the river for a couple of days with a bottle of wine and a good book, or as ambitious as walking the length of the Bicentennial Trail. The point is to know what you want to do, where you want to go, what experiences you hope to have, and plan accordingly.

Planning sites and routes

Topographical maps, showing height above sea level via contour lines, campsites, roads, four-wheel-drive trails, paths, tracks, huts and other physical features, are a good place to start. These maps are generally available from national parks authorities. Much information can be gleaned from these maps: terrain topology, the paths of rivers and creeks, the location of access trails as well as the nearest houses, villages or towns in case of emergency or for stocking up on supplies.

These maps, however, describe little of the underlying terrain and vegetation types, and can sometimes be deceptive in describing cliffed areas. What looks to be a few short metres to the creek to fetch some water for the billy could turn out to be a first-hand introduction to base jumping without a parachute. Especially if those few metres happen to consist of dense, impenetrable scrub obscuring the location of the clifftop. It is often best to research the area to be visited through books and other publications, the national parks authorities, locals, friends, clubs or societies. These sources can also provide information on the local climatic conditions, whether it is hot, cool, wet, dry, subject to floods or fires, high winds and so forth. For budding botanists and naturalists there may also be information on vegetation and animal species to be found in the area. An intimate knowledge of terrain also helps in estimating travel times, as well as identifying impenetrable obstacles which may not be picked up on the topographical map you have with you.

It is a good idea to have several alternative camping sites marked out on the map in case the preferred site is already overrun with campers or turns out to be situated next to a mosquito-infested creek. And if you press on a bit further, you never know, there may be an even better campsite waiting undiscovered around the next bend.

Transport

Plan for all your transportation needs carefully. Going outdoors in cars or four-wheel-drive vehicles is the best way to start an interest in camping or bushwalking—it is easy to organise, there is plenty of space to pack all the food and gear, and room for passengers. Also, driving to camp minimises the walking that may be required to transport the gear to the campsite. Driving does raise additional issues though, such as which roads and trails are open in the national parks, where fuel can be bought and at what times, where to park, security, and how the costs of driving are to be shared among the group. For your own peace of mind, these issues should be resolved as early as possible.

Many sites that are established and maintained by national parks authorities usually have space and access trails for vehicles to park right next to the camp. As more experience is gained, campers can easily discern what equipment is truly necessary to bring along—on more self-contained trips it becomes vital to minimise weight and encumbrances. Leaving open the option of vehicular camping, however, allows far greater freedom in the choice of location, equipment and gear, and requires little skill in packing backpacks for optimal efficiency.

Weather

Even the best plans can be foiled by weather. While handling all sorts of weather conditions is an integral part of the outdoors experience, there is no need to press on with the trip if it is predicted that conditions will be really foul. Be aware of weather reports in the region and have a backup plan or arrangement, perhaps even cancellation if things look grim close to the set-off date. Weather reports can also be used to help to determine any additional equipment and provisions (such as extra thermal underwear, food, ice axes and so forth) that should be included for your trip.

Permits and fires

Before setting out it is wise to check with the relevant authorities the condition of potential campsites, whether the intended campsites and national parks are open, whether camping permits are required and fees enforced, and especially in the summer months, if fire bans are in operation. Campfires may be banned at *all* times in some ecologically-sensitive areas, so it is a good idea to check this first before bringing along the spit-roast.

Practice pitches

It makes a lot of sense to become as fully acquainted as possible with your equipment before setting out, and this means knowing the very basic skills of how to pitch the tent and light the portable stove. This can be practised without too much embarrassment in a backyard or, if no room there, a local park or reserve, and provides a good opportunity to sort out any difficulties in ideal conditions. (Note: learning how to pitch a tent in blinding snow at night on a rocky alpine outcrop is not 'ideal conditions'.)

Notification

Once your itinerary or plan for the camp trip has been established, leave a copy of this information with a reliable relative or friend, including the names of the participants, the intended routes taken, the estimated travel times and resources carried. An 'overdue' time should also be included, beyond which time search-and-rescue authorities should be notified. This central contact person should be known and accessible to the families of all the camp participants to prevent undue panic and false alarms. See page 116 for a sample Walker Intention Form.

Camp craft

Selecting a campsite, organising the tents, making a good fire, dealing with water and waste while at the same time minimising the impact on the environment, these are all basic skills that everyone should know when staying out in the bush. For a summary, see the Code of Walking and Camping reproduced on pages 42–45.

Campsite location

When establishing a place to set up camp, priority should be given to safety and comfort. You should consider the following aspects when selecting a campsite:

- Is there ready access to fresh water?
- Is the site large enough to pitch all the tents?
- Is there a fireplace and/or wood if not carrying a fuel stove?
- Is it sheltered from wind and rain?
- If it rains, will runoff water flow away from the site rather than into it?
- Is there a risk of falling tree branches? (Redgums by river banks are especially susceptible to shedding massive branches without notice.)
- Is it relatively flat and free of rocks, roots and shrubs?
- Is it free of ants' nests, mosquitoes, insects and other pests?
- Are there other campers?
- Will the wind blow smoke, embers and ashes over the tent?
- Is there a good view, or other aesthetic quality?
- Is the ground hard and dry (and so won't deteriorate quickly)?

Campfire tips

- Never leave the fire unattended.
- Do not place wet or porous rocks near the fireplace as they may explode, shattering fragments over a wide area.
- Some types of rock can make a good fuel, however, and produce long-lasting coals for cooking or warmth. Examples are oil-shale that can be found in abundance in some areas in the upper Capertee and Wolgan Rivers in the Wollemi National Park. In Kanangra-Boyd National Park there is a coal seam which has been used by campers for decades.
- For obvious reasons, don't light a fire on peat grounds. This is outlawed in all Australian states where peat grounds exist.
- A reflector on one side of the fire can act as a vacuum, channelling smoke upwards as well as reflecting heat back to the camp group. Any tall person can be employed as a smoke-channeller if nothing else is available.
- Positioning the fire a few metres from a large rock or boulder will allow you to sit between the rock and the fire, making you warmer still.

Water is one essential resource that cannot be carried in large quantities, so supplies of fresh, clean water close to camp is a preferable option. Unfortunately, with the exception of Tasmania, Australia cannot claim to be blessed with an abundance of reliable clean water. Constant cyclical periods of drought diminish water levels and the ability of watercourses to flush themselves out. A classic example is the alarmingly low water levels often experienced in the Nattai River in the southern Blue Mountains, leading to stagnation.

In addition, fertilisers and insecticides from farms, sewerage from urban residences, industrial waste, as well as the poor hygienic standards of some campers and bushwalkers have compromised many of the once-pristine waterways in Australia's national parks. While there are still many clean watercourses, if there is any doubt about the water quality it is better to boil the water for ten minutes, or to use a purifier system, rather than risk suffering the effects of imbibing *Giardia* parasites, *Cryptosporidium* or other nasty bacteria.

That said, there is no need to set up camp as close to the watercourse as possible. Heavy rain can raise the level of rivers and creeks by metres in only a few hours, and some waterways may be a breeding ground for flies, mosquitoes or other biting insects; or they may act as an important water source for local fauna which may be scared away by the presence of tents and campsite noises. Further, setting up camp away from the edge of the water source may help in preventing accidental polluting of the waterway from camp run-off. If camping away from water, such as on a high ridge or arid location, water will have to be carried into camp. The most practical containers are clear plastic soft drink bottles or collapsible wine bladders.

Campsites should also be selected for the quality of shelter they provide against rain, wind and electrical storms. For this reason, camping on top of a hill, or on the windward side can create difficulties. Camping in valley floors or hollows can provide protection from the wind, but can be problematic in that they attract moisture from the surrounding hills, are colder and, under clear skies, can collect frosts. Ideally, the camp will be placed in a hollow on a rise or hill, leeward of prevailing winds and safe from ground moisture and water run-off. Unless you are conducting electrical experiments, avoid camping under single trees in otherwise featureless plains or on hillocks. Lightning always seeks the shortest possible route between the ground and the charged particles in storm clouds, and will use the tree, tents and the human beings sheltering inside as conductors.

The Lowepro Photo Trekker AW can safely carry two professional camera outfits.

The One Planet Mistress is a strong, medium sized 50-litre backpack.

The Avocet Vertech altimeter watch is useful for navigation and weather forecasting.

4

5

6

4   The Guardian Sweetwater Plus filtration
    system can be used almost anywhere.

5   Airing the tent fly keeps it fresh and dry.

6   Self-supporting tents need no pegs or
    guy ropes for erection.

Prominent features on the horizon make excellent cross-references when aligning maps.

The Eureka Bike & Hike tent weighs under 2kg, yet sleeps two people.

The turquoise waters of Western River Cove on Kangaroo Island, SA.

10 Drinking water should always be
    obtained from flowing water sources.

11 Always beware of soft crumbling
    rock near cliff tops, especially after
    recent rain.

2 Outback camping requires an especially high degree of self-sufficiency due to the isolation.

3 This perfect campsite—shady, grassy, and protected—is on the New England tableland.

4 Tasmania has a host of high-altitude lakes beside which to camp.

15 Abseiling, especially into canyons, can be a tough but rewarding experience.

16 A hearty meal at the end of a day's walking is one of the joys of camping.

17 In camp and cooking a meal beside Lake Yarrunga, Morton National Park, NSW.

8 A classic old A-frame tent with steel frames,
   used throughout the 1970s.

9 Fly fishing in Tasmania has boomed since
   the introduction of trout to the island's
   river systems.

0 Fishing can supplement an evening meal.
   Murramurang National Park, NSW.

21 Carrying a heavy overnight pack can double the time it takes to climb mountains.

22 Taking a break while mountain biking through Tasmania.

23 The interior of some two-person tents are surprisingly spacious for their light weight.

Trees that have many dead branches, or have a tendency to drop branches in winds, whether dead or alive, are also best given a wide berth. The ground beneath the tents will preferably be hardy, flat, not too damp, and free of gnarled roots, holes, nests and low-cover vegetation.

Camp layout

Having established a site to camp there is further skill required in positioning the tents, toilets, fires, and cooking and washing areas for hygiene, safety and comfort. The following tips in camp layout can help to improve a good site, or make the best of a bad position:

- a southerly tent alignment allows the morning sun to rise across the tent rather than straight through it
- an open vista can funnel a breeze and clear away insects
- always use a groundsheet inside the tent
- if necessary, a tent can be storm-proofed against heavy winds and rains by securing additional guylines (supporting ropes), waterproofing seals and exposed hemlines beforehand, and reinforcing all stakes and pegs with rubber bands or shock cord. This allows lines to 'give' a little before blowing down.
- know the vulnerability of your tent, especially seams and hems around the entrance where water may seep through. If on sloping ground, keep the vulnerable parts pointing downhill, away from any water run-off
- if the ground is damp or boggy, don't pitch the tents close together. During heavy rains, the tents will direct water onto each other like a guttering system
- keep the fire/cooking area away and downwind from the tents
- use toilet facilities if provided, otherwise develop your own site at least 100 metres away from the camp and water sources.

Lighting fires

While not a necessary ingredient to a successful camp, a good campfire can nonetheless provide warmth, a social focal point and a place to cook. Campfires need not be large to be effective for cooking. Be aware that in some regions, such as the high alpine regions in Tasmania, fires are banned because of the risk of causing irreversible ecological damage. Some burned scrubs take a long time to regenerate; some never do.

Use an existing fireplace where possible. If there is none, choose a place at least three metres away from tents and flammable vegetation—which is a legal requirement in many Australian states—preferably on bare ground or a sandy creek bed. Before deciding on the location of the fire, make a note of the wind so that embers will not be blowing on your expensive tent or on dry leaf litter.

A rock perimeter is unnecessary and is discouraged by national parks authorities. It is a mystery why the practice became so prevalent. There are four disadvantages to having rocks around a fire:

- disturbing rocks undermines habitats for insects that shelter under them
- rocks block heat, thus requiring a larger fire
- it is more difficult for longer pieces of burning timber to be in contact with the centre of the fire. Consequently, the fire burns inefficiently
- river rocks can explode because of the heated expanding gases from the moisture trapped in them.

Form a base of dry leaf and grass tinder and then lay small twigs on this in a pyramid formation. Light with a match or lighter. Larger twigs and branches found on nearby ground can be added quickly as the fire gathers strength. Placing larger pieces of wood on the fire early on will soon yield a pile of hot coals that will make a good stove. Lighting a fire in wet conditions requires more skill and patience: searching in the lee of trees and rocks for dry kindling, whittling wet sticks to expose drier sections beneath, fanning the fire vigorously to keep up its intensity—even using the old kerosene tricks or solid fuel tablets is a good fallback.

Always extinguish all fires before leaving the campsite by dousing thoroughly with water, or covering completely with sand or earth if there is no water available.

Cleaning and washing

Cleanliness may be next to godliness, but the bush has its own religions. If you are so dirty that you must use soap or toothpaste, it is advised that you do so at least 50 metres away from streams, scattering the used water on the ground so it can be filtered by the soil before returning to the river system.

Any water used for washing-up should likewise be kept clear of rivers and streams. Detergents and soaps do not get along very well with local fauna and flora, and biodegradable soaps are preferable to other varieties. A handful of coarse sand can work wonders on a blackened billy if the scourer was left behind. The less left in the billy to wash up, the better, so good hygiene and sanitation is an excuse to put on a few extra kilos.

Waste disposal
Ideally, carry only foods and other materials that have few disposable parts or little unnecessary packaging. Use any rubbish bins provided at the campsite, carrying home whatever cannot fit. Don't bury any rubbish.

Toilet training
If there are no facilities available, use a trowel to dig a hole at least 15 centimetres deep and at least 100 metres away from the campsite, and cover properly when you are done. Use bio-friendly toilet paper and burn afterwards if possible before covering up to aid decomposition.

Water quality

In the bush there are four potential dangers with drinking creek water: chemical pollutants, protozoa and larger parasites, bacteria, and viruses.

Chemical pollutants
Chemicals in water could include inorganic contaminants such as arsenic and other heavy metals, or organic toxins such as fertilisers and pesticides. In general, it is a bad idea to trust any purification system to remove these pollutants, as even small quantities could ruin your day in a hurry. The good news is that water sources in the bush are seldom contaminated with appreciable levels of toxic chemicals. Take a good look at the stream you're about to get water from. Are there fish swimming in it? Is there algae on the rocks? Yabbies on the bottom? Insects skimming the surface? Plants growing along the banks? If yes, the water is probably non-toxic, chemically speaking. If you're hiking in the desert, though, and a trickle of water etching a groove in the rock is bubbling sulphur from its barren depths, you would do well to avoid it.

Protozoa and larger parasites

There are a number of parasites, both multicellular and unicellular, that live in water. The most common ones in Australia are *Giardia* and *Cryptosporidium*, and information on these is provided on pages 64-65. A good filter will remove both parasites, and boiling will kill them. Iodine is a reasonable second choice, but is a bit chancy in water carrying *Cryptosporidium*, especially if the water is cold.

Bacteria

Bacteria are the second smallest pathogens in water. All types of bacteria are sensitive to iodine treatment, are killed by water–boiling, and are removed by good filters.

Viruses

The smallest parasites are viruses. In true wilderness areas, pathogenic viruses are seldom found in water, but the odds increase with population density and poor sanitation practices. Filters that have an iodine matrix will kill viruses, and iodine treatment will also work. Boiling is the most reliable way to kill viruses.

Methods of purification

The oldest and cheapest method of purifying water is to boil it. Boiling for five minutes will kill any biological hazards you could expect to find. Most pathogens are actually long dead by the time the water boils, but the full five-minute boil will get them all. However, be warned that boiling water will *not* neutralise chemical pollutants.

Chemical purification involves the use of iodine or chlorine to kill the nasties in the water. This method is lightweight and relatively inexpensive, but will not neutralise chemical toxins. Abide strictly by the quantities stipulated on the bottle label or the packet. In addition, you must make sure that water at 25°C sits for 20–30 minutes with iodine in it in order for purification to take place. If the water is colder, you will need to let it sit longer—possibly overnight for cold stream water. Warm the water against your body or even on your stove if you want it to be purified faster. Once the appropriate time has elapsed, the taste of iodine can be neutralised with a small amount of ascorbic acid (vitamin C). Used properly, iodine will kill most protozoa and all bacteria and viruses in water.

Common Tree Frog

3

Advanced Camping Techniques: For the rugged solo adventurer in all of us

Charting new territory

After you've relied on a guidebook to introduce you to some longer overnight walks, you may wish to venture out to a destination of your own choosing, following your own itinerary. Maybe not the full length of the Kokoda Trail just yet, or a winter traverse through Antarctica, but there are many more modest challenges awaiting you. The best method for planning a route is to purchase the 1:25 000 scale maps that cover the area you want to walk and work out a route along the fire trails, walking tracks and negotiable routes that go the most scenic way to where you intend to visit.

Distance
The average walking speed on dirt in moderately hilly country is about 3 km/h, so try not to plan day trips longer than about 20 kilometres unless you are in Olympic training or the terrain is predominantly flat. This will leave you plenty of time for rest breaks, sightseeing, exploring and unexpected delays. Ridge and plateau walking is the fastest, as a good momentum can be maintained both ways.

Time

The best and simplest tip one can follow is to leave early, about 6 or 7 am. If everything goes according to plan, you will arrive at your destination early. If things don't, you still have time up your sleeve to deal with problems. One of the main problems with exploring virgin bush is running out of daylight hours. Learn to recognise features on topographical maps, as this allows the pace of progress to be checked. Try to plan routes on established walking tracks at first before accumulating enough experience to walk through the bush.

Packing techniques

The body

Wearing a pack causes the torso to lean forward. The spine has to carry all of the upper bodyweight. The curves, especially the lower or lumbar curve, are vital in absorbing the shock of vertical movements such as stepping or jumping down. It is essential that your natural posture be changed as little as possible when carrying a pack.

The last thing to note about the body is that only areas well-padded by muscle are able to comfortably bear pressure from the pack harness. The upper buttocks extending out to the sides are best suited to bear pressure at the hip level. Either side of the spine on the upper back and the front of the chest also has sufficient muscle cover to serve as load platforms. Near our spine the lumbar region is poorly padded.

The vertical spacing between the hip harness and the shoulder harness must match the torso length of the wearer. If the pack is too long the shoulder harness won't bed down on the shoulders properly as all the weight will be carried by the hips. With a short pack it is the hip harness that fails to sit down where it's needed.

The pack bag

Again, the shape of the pack bag and the way it is packed affects upright stability and the dynamic balance of the walker. If a simple box-shaped pack is placed on the back, there is an automatic tendency to lean forward. However, by moving the lower part of this box pack up to the top, the need for forward body tilt is reduced. This is because the new shape puts the pack weight (acting from the pack centre of gravity) closer to directly above the footprint. A more natural posture is possible. What's more, for top-opening packs, which the majority are, the wider mouth makes the packing of and access to gear trouble-free.

The pack bag should be symmetrical in order to maximise lateral, side-to-side stability. For dynamic balance, the arms need to swing freely, counterbalancing leg movements. Practical issues such as moving easily through scrub require clearance, especially at shoulder height. Put all this together and the back view of the bag shape is chest width at the top, broadening a little to hip width at the bottom so there are no protruding parts to catch on vegetation and rocks.

Packing a backpack

Although this may at first seem like a straightforward exercise, the adoption of a few simple tips can prevent that sore back feeling walkers often get upon returning from a camp.

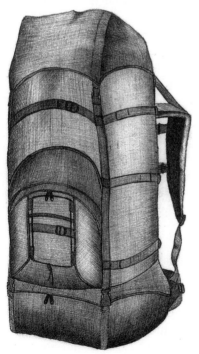

1   Use a checklist to ensure everything is taken. See page 115 for a sample list.
2   Compact, heavy items such as water, fuel or food should be packed against the frame but a little lower than shoulder height in order to lower the centre of gravity.
3   Soft items should be packed behind the harness. Conversely, sharp objects should be packed away from the back.
4   Items such as tents, cooking equipment, and maps can be shared between party members. Don't double-up where only one will do; for example, why take two can-openers?
5   Keep essentials such as your compass and torch in the back pocket. Lunches and other snacks should be packed at the top for easy access. This will also prevent them from being crushed.
6   Food should be packed in such a way that there is no danger of leakage.

7 Sleeping bags should be wrapped in plastic for extra proofing in case of creek crossings and rain.

8 Poles and sleeping mats should be packed internally where possible. Only as a last resort should important equipment be strapped externally on the pack. This will avoid losing it or becoming entangled in overhanging branches, and will ensure the balanced design of the pack.

9 If there is space left over, avoid the temptation to fill it up.

10 Always pack an extra night's food, just for contingency purposes.

Navigation techniques

Navigation in the bush follows the same basic principles as navigating the streets. We use maps to identify location, destination and routes; we use natural features in the terrain such as mountains, streams and rivers as signs to assess where we are at any given moment and to decide upon appropriate routes. In negotiating city streets there is usually no need to know the exact direction or bearing—north-east, south, south-west—as the networks of streets themselves can act as a guide. In the bush, however, there are no such easy networks of roads—there may not even be a recognisable trail—so knowing how to read a map and relate it to the direction headed, whether independently or via a compass, becomes vital. As experience is gained, navigation starts to become second nature, allowing ventures into unknown wilderness without fuss or bother. In an emergency, a good navigator will know the easiest and quickest routes out of the bush to where help can be found; a skill that could save lives.

Maps

Maps are probably the single most useful piece of equipment you can have when venturing out in the wilderness. Only water is more essential. The most commonly used type of maps for campers and bushwalkers are topographical maps, which are produced from aerial photographs and are usually very reliable–although some mistakes may arise because of surveying errors or because of out-dating.

General tourist maps are adequate for planning purposes but tell next to nothing about the lay of the land and so are virtually useless for navigating in the bush. Some maps overlay topography with aerial photographs to give some idea of terrain type and vegetation, which can be very useful. Depending on the scale, however, these maps can sometimes be unclear, and are generally not available for many locations.

The distinguishing feature of topographical maps is the use of contour lines to delineate vertical height above sea level. Each contour line refers to a specific height, and the difference in vertical height between contour lines is known as the contour interval of the map.

Purchasing maps

Maps are produced by each state department of lands, such as the Land Information Office in New South Wales (formerly the Central Mapping Authority). In addition there is a Commonwealth department called AUSLIG (formerly NATMAP) that produces AUSMAP 1:100 000 maps that have quite a comprehensive coverage.

Detailed information on the various state government mapping departments and their products is given on pages 117–121. Good outlets for maps are national park visitor centres and large camping/disposals retailers.

Map name

Most people prefer to use the map name rather than the map number that places it within the Commonwealth 1:100 000 map grid system. The map name is a 'human readable' name to use when referring to a particular map. Each one is unique and is usually relevant in some way to the landscape it is depicting. For example, the VICMAP 'Genoa' has the Genoa River on it.

Grid reference

Bushwalkers often use a six-digit grid reference to identify features to fellow walkers; for example, when planning over the telephone or via email. It employs the one-kilometre grid, starting with the horizontal axis. The first two numbers indicate the vertical line on the left of the point while the third number indicates how far to the next vertical line east. For example, if the point is midway between the two lines, then five is used; if it's 90 per cent of the way to the next vertical line, then nine is used; and so on. Another way of representing this third digit is the number of hundred metres from the left vertical line.

The second set of three digits in the six-digit grid reference number represent the vertical axis, using the same methodology. Thus, it is possible to pinpoint a locality to inside a 100-metre square, close enough for visual sighting and verification.

When using a grid reference, it is useful to indicate which map you are using. For example, you can use 'Cunningham Gap-403978' to indicate Mount Cordeux on the Cunninghams Gap 1:25 000 topographical map.

Map number

In Australia, all topographical maps are part of the Commonwealth AUSMAP 1:100 000 system. Hence, they are each allocated a four-digit map number. For example, TASMAP's 'Razorback' map is 4422.

The second set of Roman numerals indicates the quadrant of the 1:100 000 map. The quadrants start with I, being the north-east, rotating clockwise to IV being the north-west. This may seem counter-intuitive. Just remember that the Australian Map Grid is left-handed, not right-handed—Australia is in the southern hemisphere.

The last character is always either an S or N, and this indicates the north or south half of the quadrant. The result of this is that a 1:100 000 map is composed of eight separate 1:25 000 maps.

The compass

The compass can be an extremely useful tool in navigation. Combined with a good topographical map, a compass allows:

- the calculation of bearings (direction) that can accurately assist you in obtaining your position
- guided travel even when the destination is hidden or obscured by natural features such as mists, valleys or hills, when navigating featureless terrain
- the location of other features
- you to get 'back on track' when you have veered off-course.

When using the compass it is important to remember that it should be kept as horizontal as possible, to allow the floating needle to move most easily to magnetic north within the 'housing' that the needle floats around in, and to avoid taking bearings close to magnetic disturbances.

Aligning the map

A map, by itself, is not useful as a navigational device unless it is correctly aligned or oriented. This means rotating the map so that the north pointer on the map is actually pointing north, therefore placing ground features on the land in the correct alignment to your perspective. This can be done by simple observation, if distinguishing features are readily apparent. It can also be done with a compass by following these steps:

- place the compass on the map so that the travel arrow points to true north
- rotate the housing so that the orienting arrow points to magnetic north
- then rotate the map so that the magnetic arrow lies over the orienting arrow.

The map is now oriented correctly and should match your perspective view.

Taking a bearing

This is a useful technique in navigating towards unseen destinations, and can be done with a compass in three basic steps. While often learnt in a mechanical fashion, there is a certain logic present. Taking bearings requires a little practice to do quickly and properly. It is also easy to make mistakes and end up travelling in exactly the opposite direction intended. The steps to master are:

- Locate the line of direction to travel. Place the longer edge of the compass base plate (or one of the direction lines on this plate) across both your present location and your destination on the map. Be sure the travel arrow points to your destination.
- Set the north/south lines. Turn the compass housing dial around until the north/south lines line up with the gridlines on the map. Be sure the orienting arrow points north. Correct for magnetic declination by twisting the orienting arrow a little further to magnetic north as marked on the map.
- Find your bearing. Take the compass from the map and hold it out flat in front of your stomach, with the travel arrow pointing away from you. Turn yourself until the compass needle lies on top of the orienting arrow. The travel arrow now points directly to your destination. The bearing in degrees can be read from the dial on the rim of the compass housing above the travel arrow.

While moving along a fixed bearing, take regular sightings from obvious landmarks in your path rather than walking with your head bent over your compass continuously, making sure the compass needle is aligned correctly. Shorter distances between sightings allow for the most accurate routes, so long as bearings are checked after each sighting point.

Norths

You should be aware of the three types of north:

1 **True north** is the geographic axis about which our planet spins. This is quite irrelevant for walking purposes.
2 **Magnetic north** is the north that compasses point to. It's quite an angle from true north because of the alignment of the earth's magnetic field. What's more confusing is that magnetic north is slowly moving by approximately one degree every decade. This necessitates a variation compensation that depends upon the year and location. All topographical maps contain a magnetic variation diagram which gives you the appropriate conversion information to enable taking an accurate bearing. At present, in the eastern states of Australia, magnetic declination can lie between eight and 13 degrees east; in Western Australia it can range between −4 or +4 degrees. It is predicted that in the very distant future, the earth's magnetic field could invert altogether so that north becomes south, and vice versa.
3 **Grid north** is the alignment of the artificial grid that dissects each map in one-kilometre increments. It is a close approximation to true north.

Determining position

The ability to determine your exact position on a map is another useful navigational skill, and an invaluable one if you should ever become lost. Position can be determined accurately by taking a bearing towards a nearby feature, or two features if you are uncertain which feature you may be standing alongside. To determine your position on the map follow these steps:

- physically aim the compass at the observable feature as accurately as possible
- while keeping the travel arrow trained on the feature, rotate the compass housing until its north/south lines are matched with the magnetic needle
- place the compass on the map and correct for magnetic declination by rotating the housing slightly so that the orienting arrow points to grid north while the magnetic needle points at magnetic north

- place the compass so that one edge of the base plate lies on the observed feature, then rotate the compass entirely so that its north/south lines and the orienting arrow are parallel to the gridlines
- draw a line from the feature on the map down the side of the base plate.

You will be somewhere along this line so drawn. If you are on a river or other feature, simply see where this line hits the feature for your position. If you are at all unsure as to your whereabouts, repeat the process a second time with another observable feature. Where the two lines so drawn intersect, that is your position. A third bearing and line can deliver even greater accuracy. And if this doesn't appear to be working, it is time to switch on your Global Positioning System (GPS).

Basic navigation tips

- Check which end of the magnetic needle points north before taking bearings. This is usually the red end, or the end with a luminous tip.
- Practice taking bearings and reading maps in familiar locations before venturing out into unknown territory.
- Failing to correct for magnetic declination can lead to large errors over long distances. An easy way to remember how to adjust bearings for declination is to memorise the rhyme: 'East is Least' (subtract the declination from the bearing when the declination is east) and 'West is Best' (add the declination to the bearing when the declination is west).
- While every person should have their own compass, having two or more for a party is adequate.
- Don't rely on compass bearings taken near magnetic disturbances, electrical currents or steel surfaces, or where known natural iron-laden rock deposits are nearby. This includes being near torches, knives, guns, sheds, power lines and some digital watches. The heavier the iron, the further away bearings should be made. This could be a metre away from a knife or axe; 10–20 metres away from a steel shed.
- Store the compass away from electrical and magnetic fields when not in use, otherwise it can become reverse magnetised and point south.
- Keep maps waterproof by wrapping them inside a plastic bag or coating them in a waterproofing substance. If doing the latter, ensure you can still write on the map with a pen or pencil.
- Carry spare pens and pencils for calculating bearings and estimating your position.

Using a GPS with a topographical map

The combination of an accurate topographical map and a reliable GPS unit is almost infallible. In fact, it's so effective that some hard-core bushwalking purists might consider it spoils the fun, analogous to entering in the cheat codes on a computer game. However, for long expeditions in very remote trackless regions such as the Kimberley, one can never have too much data. A GPS system might even save a life.

Topographical maps commonly used by bushwalkers contain metric grids that are marked every 1000 metres. These metric grids are known as UTM (Universal Transverse Mercator), and are so convenient that GPS receivers can be set to solve for position in these coordinates. The UTM grids are usually offset slightly in angle from the map geodetic grid. Because of convergence of the meridians of longitude, the map is narrower at the top than at the bottom. The UTM measurements are called 'eastings' and 'northings', which are in fact distances east and north from the UTM reference lines.

For more information on how the GPS works, see pages 6-7.

Entering waypoints into a GPS unit

GPS units allow perhaps a few dozen waypoints to be entered as a continuous route. Each location on a route is called a waypoint. For each waypoint, the location can be entered anywhere, even when planning your trip at home. The route for the trip is then set up to proceed from one waypoint to the next. Current GPS receivers also allow the route to be traced backwards. This avoids entering a new reverse route for the way back.

At the staging area of your walk—usually the car—take a GPS fix, then enter the local position. Once the route is chosen, the direction and distance to the next waypoint will be displayed. Since the initial values were entered from the map, the location will vary from the GPS fix at that location. Selective Availability (see page 7) will also slightly corrupt the position fix. GPS fixes should be logged into a notebook for all important locations. Later, you can update the trail coordinate notes for another trip.

As you travel along the route, the receiver will indicate the direction to the next waypoint. Since the waypoint location may be subject to error, careful interpretation is needed to avoid blunders. If time permits, a new GPS fix should be taken at each waypoint to update the coordinates.

If you are wandering off the track, you can estimate which way the track is, since your motion allows the GPS to compute the direction and speed you are moving. The direction to the track can be estimated as you head towards it, or the direction to one of the track waypoints may be followed to intercept it.

In spite of the convenience of GPS, a compass and map should always be taken in case the GPS receiver or its batteries fail. Whenever the GPS track is noted, the compass bearing should be checked in case you may have to rely upon it later because of a GPS receiver failure.

How to find your way without a compass or GPS

Orienteering with the use of only a map is simply a matter of pattern recognition which will develop with practice. Learn to recognise features on the map using the contour lines and the detailed legend. With time you'll be able to obtain the following information about your trip even before you embark:

- vegetation density
- which streams you'll be crossing
- purity of the water
- altitude gain/loss
- how steep the terrain is
- where good lunch spots lie
- the best lookouts and campsites
- the fastest way out in case of an emergency.

While this may seem a little ambitious, one can infer certain information from the details given, even if the information isn't directly supplied. For example, if there is no official lookout marked, you know that a high, open point will provide panoramic views. Similarly, a stream is likely to be drinkable if you can trace its origin and are sure there is no human development contained within the boundaries of its watersheds.

Confirmation of position by alternative means

Experienced walkers will develop secondary navigational skills that are more tangible than simply having a good sense of direction. They employ simple observation and awareness of their surroundings. Another consequence of developing alternative navigational skills is that reliance on a compass or GPS is reduced. Of course it is wise to still use them but when they fail, someone who can navigate without them is less likely to feel stranded or challenged.

It is sometimes necessary to rely on an alternative means to confirm your position: for example, when a magnetic anomaly misaligns a compass bearing. A good habit to get into is to always double-check using another means, regardless of whether your primary equipment is working.

The sun and moon

Advanced navigation techniques can commence with the simplest and most reliable of indicators—our closest star. If you want to head east in the afternoon and you're squinting, there's something wrong. We know that the sun and moon rise in the east and set in the west. Accordingly, we know where the sun should be in the sky at a particular time of the day. As the earth rotates 15 degrees every hour, the height of the sun above the horizon can be used to determine the time since sunrise, or more importantly, the time till sunset. This can be applied to the moon, or any celestial body that is near the celestial equator.

The stars

The vast majority of Australians reside in urban environments. The cities we live in generate a lot of light pollution which, coupled with smog, washes out the colour and brilliance of the stars. Consequently, most people know little about finding directions from the stars. In fact, most people know little about the stars at all. This wasn't always the case, however. While ancient people didn't know how far away the stars were or how hot they were, they knew their patterns intimately.

Finding directions from the stars is a much more accurate method than using the sun or the moon. The first step is to determine a reference direction. We have four methods to choose from:

1 South can be found by measurement from recognised star patterns. True south is the point on the horizon directly below the South Celestial Pole.
2 East or west can be found directly from bright stars near the celestial equator as they rise and set.
3 The directions of the rising and setting of bright stars away from the celestial equator can be learned and used directly as a navigational tool. Unfortunately, these directions are affected by latitude. This method was very popular before the invention of the compass.
4 Observing the apparent motion of the stars.

The Southern Cross is probably the best-known constellation in the southern hemisphere. It is highest in the evening sky from March to September. Several methods and variations are possible to find south from the Southern Cross. Beta Centauri is the closest of the two pointers, and south is usually halfway between this star and the Cross.

Orion is well known worldwide. It is visible in the evening sky from November to May. The belt and sword of Orion is otherwise known as 'The Pot' because of its resemblance to a saucepan. Mintaka is the star of Orion's belt furthest from the sword. It is within one degree of the celestial equator, so it rises and sets due east and west respectively.

When it is directly overhead, the handle of the pot (Orion's sword) points north/south. When the pot is not directly overhead, north or south can be found by projecting a line parallel to the sword of Orion for 90 degrees from Mintaka. On the sword side of Mintaka this would locate the South Celestial Pole.

The best way to observe the apparent motion of the stars is to use a fixed sight, and keep the eye very still. The best way to keep the eye still is to lie down on your back in a comfortable position with your head comfortably supported. The sight could be a stiff stick supported rigidly so one end is overhead, or a protrusion of rock from an overhead cliff. Trees and branches make poor sights as they move and sway in the slightest breeze.

It takes only a few minutes to observe the direction of motion of the stars. Note carefully the position of a star very near the sight. Wait a few minutes or until the motion is apparent to observe the motion of the star, but do not move your head. It is worth mentioning here that stars move very slowly near the celestial poles. This is only useful as a 'sense of direction' aid. It too is complicated by the observer's latitude and is subject to errors if a star is chosen that is low in the sky. Always pick a star high in the sky or greater than your latitude above the horizon.

If it is impractical to sight a star directly overhead, the following method may be suitable. Observe the motions of stars near the horizon roughly 90 degrees apart. Where the stars either move very slowly, or move parallel to the horizon, may be either north or south. Where the stars rise steeply from the horizon is obviously east, and where they set steeply is west. The angle of movement for stars at east or west equals 90 degrees minus the observer's latitude. For example, at 35 degrees south, a star at the east will rise at an angle of 55 degrees from the horizon. The angle always 'leans' towards the equator. This is a very rough method, and will provide 'sense of direction' information only, not accurate directions. It is also of diminishing value as latitude increases. For example, at the poles, the stars on the horizon simply move parallel to the horizon.

Makeshift compasses
What happens if you've forgotten your compass or you drop it down a cliff? There are several alternative ways to improvise and impress your friends at the same time.

1 Using the sun and a watch
One of the most renowned methods of finding north during the day uses an analogue watch. It's only applicable to the region south of the Tropic of Capricorn, which fortunately contains 95 per cent of Australia's premium bushwalking regions. Align the 12 on the watch-face with the sun. Then mentally halve the angle between the hour hand and the 12. This direction is roughly north.

For this method to work accurately, the watch must be set to Eastern Standard Time and not daylight saving time. Daylight saving time will result in a 15-degree error to the east. If you are wearing a digital watch, you can draw the watch-face in the dirt, or somewhere else, and calculate north from there.

Unfortunately, this method can be fairly inaccurate: errors of up to 25 or 30 degrees or more are possible unless you understand the movements of the sun and can compensate for factors such as seasonal variation. The method is most accurate in the middle of the day. It loses accuracy and reliability as your latitude approaches the tropics, and is not recommended for use there.

2 Using a stick
Another simple but effective method is to plant a stick in the ground before midday and mark the position and length of its shadow. Periodically plot the length of the shadow until it is at a minimum, then continue for a similar amount of time afterwards. The shadow is at its minimum length at noon. The line through the tip of the shadow, sometime before midday, and the tip of the shadow the same time after midday, will point west/east. The fact that it is the same time each side of midday is important because the tip of the shadow will describe a curve on the ground and not a straight east/west line.

3 Using a stick and a watch

If an accurate watch set to Eastern Standard Time is available, the stick used to generate the shadow need not be vertical. Simply plot the positions of the shadow tips at the same time each side of noon. Without the watch, it is important to get the tip of the stick vertically over the base so that shadow lengths can be used to determine equal time before and after midday.

Both these methods are reasonably accurate but are limited in that they can be used only once per day. Using a vertical stick and equal shadow lengths has no inherent error, but may be subject to significant personal error, such as how vertical the stick is and measuring shadow lengths. Using a watch is subject to an inherent error due to position within a time zone (+/- 30 minutes); however, the effect of this on the accuracy of the direction determined depends on latitude, and the length of time used each side of midday. Generally, using a watch will give acceptably small errors if used for at least one to two hours each side of midday. The shadow stick method will work anywhere in the world but takes time to do. These methods are most useful if applied at a location where good visibility of the horizon is possible so that a prominent landmark can be used for guidance once the sun is no longer visible.

4 Using a needle

If the sky is so overcast that it is not possible to ascertain the direction of the sun or moon, you might like to try to magnetise a needle, nail, or wire by stroking it repeatedly with silk and suspending it from a thread. Provided it is balanced and not influenced by the breeze, the needle will indicate the north/south alignment of the magnetic axis. Hopefully you aren't that lost that you won't know north from south. A similarly makeshift compass can be made by supporting the needle in a cork floating on water, or paper or a leaf supported by surface tension on water.

General skills

Familiar landmarks help the observer to assess direction and location. When landmarks are not visible, knowledge of the area comes into play; for example, the general direction of flow of rivers, or the fact that termites build mounds aligned north/south in northern Australia to help control internal temperature. Some flowers move to follow the sun, even when the sun is obscured behind heavy cloud. Some trees have thicker bark on the northern side of the trunk, while ridges can have thicker and wetter vegetation on their southern slopes.

4

Camping and the Law: No, you can't plead ignorance

T he last two decades have seen many government authorities use
rules and fines to encroach upon campers and camping, which was
once a free and unregulated activity. The impetus for this has been
primarily because of the pressure that national parks are suffering under
the weight of ever-increasing visitor numbers. Population growth,
increased leisure time, and the world's highest level of both urbanisation
and per capita ownership of four-wheel-drive vehicles are all factors that
contribute to the ever-growing escape to the bush.

Management policies in recent years have been largely dictated by the eco-
nomic principles of supply and demand. Pristine areas are scarce, and their
popularity ever increasing. The response by park authorities has been
two-pronged. First, large sections of national parks throughout eastern
Australia, where the demand is greatest, have been closed. Locked gates are
being constructed everywhere so that core areas are effectively out of
reach from the majority of recreational users. Second, the facilities in the
areas that remain open are upgraded and the camping grounds are actively
managed by the imposition of fees and ranger patrols. This funnelling of
holiday crowds into a few limited areas is a growing trend. One of the chief
objectives of campers is to seek relief from crowds, yet they increasingly
find themselves squeezed into densely concentrated grounds, allocated a
pre-booked numbered site, and then have to queue for the amenities.

Bans

There are many items that are prohibited in national parks. These include pets, firearms and generators. Some activities are also prohibited, which can include driving an unlicensed vehicle, lighting a campfire, littering, riding a mountain bike on a management trail, planting exotic species, removing bush rock, and cutting down native vegetation.

Familiarise yourself with the regulations of the park you are visiting. Some are generic across all parks; others are specific to one area or time of year. The most important one perhaps, is the observance of fire bans.

Code of Walking and Camping

To ensure that policy-makers aren't forced to use increasingly draconian measures it is imperative that all walkers and campers adopt and strictly follow the officially recognised Code of Walking and Camping, which is reproduced here.

Be self-reliant
- Carry with you the things you need for your comfort and safety. For shelter carry a lightweight tent or fly, or use a cave or rock overhang.
- Avoid huts except when weather conditions are really bad.

Tread softly
- Keep walking parties small in number; four to six people is ideal.
- Avoid popular areas in holiday periods when campsites are crowded.
- Use existing tracks; don't create new ones.
- On zigzag paths, don't cut corners, as this creates unsightly damage that leads to erosion.
- To minimise damage in trackless country, spread your party out and don't walk in one another's footsteps.
- Avoid easily damaged places such as peat bogs, cushion moss, swamps and fragile rock formations.
- Wade through waterlogged sections of tracks; don't create a skein of new tracks around them.
- Except in really rough terrain, wear lightweight, soft-soled walking shoes or joggers rather than heavy boots.
- Walk on rocks where possible.

- Choose a different route each time when visiting a trackless area.
- Become proficient at bush navigation. If you need to build cairns, blaze trees, place tags, break off twigs or tie knots in clumps of grass to mark your route, you are lacking in bush navigation skills. Placing signposts and permanent markers of any kind is the responsibility of the relevant land manager, such as the National Parks and Wildlife Service.

Watch your safety

- Know what to do in emergencies. Rescue operations often cause serious damage to bushland, so take care to avoid the need for rescue.
- Acquire knowledge of first aid so you know how to handle illness and injuries.
- Carry clothing and equipment to suit the worst possible conditions you are likely to encounter.
- Carry a mobile phone if you want to, but use it only for summoning aid in an emergency. Keep it switched off until needed.
- Watch for the health and safety of your group. Beware of fatigue or hypothermia affecting your group.

Pack it in, pack it out

- Don't carry glass bottles and jars, cans, drink cartons lined with aluminium foil and excess packaging. If you can't resist carrying such things, don't leave them in the bush. Remember, if you can carry a full container in, you can carry an empty one out.
- Remove all your rubbish, including food scraps, paper, plastic, aluminium foil and empty containers.
- Don't burn or bury rubbish. Burning creates pollution and buried rubbish may be dug up and scattered by wildlife. Digging also disturbs the soil, causing erosion and encouraging weeds.
- Carry a plastic bag for your rubbish. If you find litter left by irresponsible people along the track or around a campsite, please remove it. Show you care for the environment, even if others don't.
- Remove the ends off tins and flatten them.

Be hygienic

- Ensure you are at least 100 metres from campsites, streams and lakes when going to the toilet. Wait until you get out of sensitive areas such as caves and canyons before defecating or urinating. Caves and canyons are unique environments that harbour unique formations, wildlife and vegetation due to their specific micro-climates and are therefore very fragile.

- Bury all faeces and toilet paper at least 15 centimetres deep. In snow, dig through the snow first, then dig a hole in the ground.
- Carry out things that won't easily decompose, such as tampons, sanitary pads and condoms.
- Carry a lightweight plastic trowel or a large aluminium tent peg to make digging easier.

Keep water pure

- Washing dishes and bathing should be done at least 50 metres from streams as soap, detergents and food scraps are all harmful to aquatic life. Biodegradable organic soaps are preferable to commercial chemical-based varieties.
- Always swim downstream from where you draw your drinking water.

Be VERY careful with fire

- Have a fire only when you are absolutely certain you can light it with safety. A fuel stove is preferable for cooking and thermal clothing is better for warmth.
- Always use a fuel stove in places where even a tiny fire may cause permanent damage. Places where fire-lighting should be avoided include many rainforests and all alpine regions.
- Do not light a fire in hot, summer conditions, in dry windy weather, in declared fuel stove-only areas, or when there is a fire ban.
- Fire does not destroy aluminium foil, and plastics release toxic gases when burnt. Carry foil and plastics out in your pack with all your other rubbish, including your food scraps. Don't use your campfire as an incinerator.

Rules for a campfire

- In popular campsites, light your fire on a bare patch left by previous fires. Don't light it on fresh ground.
- Light your fire on bare soil or sand, well away from stumps, logs, living plants and river stones, which can explode when heated.
- Don't build a ring of stones around your campfire. This is an unnecessary and unsightly practice. Dismantle stone rings wherever you find them.
- Sweep away all leaves, grass and other flammable material for at least two metres around your campfire. Major bushfires have been caused by careless campers who didn't take this precaution.
- Burn only dead wood that has fallen to the ground. Don't break limbs from trees or shrubs.
- Keep your fire small.
- When you are finished, douse your fire thoroughly with water, even if it

appears to be out. Don't try to smother a fire by covering it with soil or sand as the coals will continue to smoulder for days. Only water will put a fire out with certainty.

- Feel the ground under the coals. If it is too hot to touch, the fire is not out. Douse it some more.
- Scatter the cold charcoal and ashes well clear of your campsite, then rake soil and leaves over the spot where your fire was. You should aim to remove all traces of it.

Protect plants and animals

- Try not to disturb wildlife. Remember, you are the trespasser.
- Give snakes a wide berth and leave them alone. They have more right to be there than you do.
- Watch where you put your feet. Walk around delicate plants.
- Don't feed birds and animals around campsites or they may become pests. Unnatural food can be harmful to many species.

Respect Aboriginal heritage

- Many places have spiritual or cultural significance for Aborigines. Treat such places with consideration and respect.
- Obtain permission from traditional landowners or the relevant land manager to visit sensitive areas.
- Leave Aboriginal relics as you find them. Don't touch paintings or rock engravings.

Be courteous to others

- The sound of radios, CD-players and similar devices is out of place in the natural environment. Leave the electronics at home.
- Ensure your behaviour and activities don't disturb or offend others.
- Camp as far away from other groups as conditions allow. Don't use another group's campfire without permission.
- Leave gates and sliprails as you find them. When you open a gate, make sure the last person through knows it has to be closed.
- Respect the rights of landholders and land managers. Don't enter private property without permission. In national parks, abide by plans of management and encourage others to do so too.

Minimal-impact bushwalking means doing nothing and leaving nothing that shows where you have been.

5

Health and Safety: Relax, it's only a flesh wound!

The Australian wilderness has a reputation, and a well-deserved one, for danger. What it doesn't have in large carnivorous animals it makes up for in extreme isolation, suffocating temperatures, and the world's most venomous snakes and spiders. But don't let minor points like these discourage you.

In many instances such direct threats are overstated. Bushwalkers can tramp through dense rainforests, across red saltbush plains and along sandy coastlines without necessarily encountering such hazardous creatures which, while being ever-present in these environments, prefer to keep out of the way rather than risk confrontation. This may be a disappointment or a blessing for those expecting to be overrun with plagues of deadly snakes and spiders upon venturing outside the city limits, but there are many more immediate perils that await the Australian camper.

Preparation

While a discussion of typical equipment can be found in Chapter One, the following items should be considered standard for health and safety:

- personal first aid kits, including high-protection sunscreen
- sunglasses and tough, appropriate clothing for the conditions expected
- a change of warm clothing regardless of expected temperature
- maps and a compass

- extra matches or a cigarette lighter in a waterproof container
- water filters/purifiers and waterproof plastic bags
- folding knife (check legality)

Advances in technology may aid the camper wishing to minimise risks in health and safety. Mobile phones, global positioning system (GPS) receivers and portable laptop computers may operate in the most isolated bush locations, providing a means of emergency communications, navigation or, via the Internet or transistor radios, providing weather updates or other local news. However, while having the potential to minimise risk, over-reliance on technological gadgets may have the unfortnuate side effect of reducing self-reliance. It can also be annoying to have the tranquil sounds of the bush broken by the harsh electronic beeps of a mobile phone, computer or radio. Most people like going to the bush to get away from these noises, and it is incredible how far sound can carry on a still, starry night. Further, while the mobile phone networks are steadily expanding and improving, it is pertinent to remember that coverage in some areas may be either limited or impaired by natural terrain.

Environmental dangers

Camping in the bush presents few direct threats to the well-prepared traveller. Far more injuries, accidents and deaths occur in day-to-day city life than in the bush. Indeed, there is a far greater risk of being hurt in the home than in the tent. The crucial difference is that, at home, resources and help are readily available if any misadventure occurs. Even with a large four-wheel-drive vehicle there is a limit to what can be brought on a camping trip, necessitating good planning and economy. Be open to the natural environment, and the risk that that entails, but don't treat your trip like an advanced SAS survival course. Enjoy nature, don't fight against it. To this end, a basic, practical knowledge of environmental dangers is extremely useful in preventing accidents and injuries, making the camping experience a more pleasant and less stressful one. Some major environmental hazards are:

- temperature extremes
- bushfires
- cyclones and high winds

- thunderstorms and lightning
- rivers and waterways
- coastal waters
- desert and semi-arid terrain
- cliffs and rocks.

The First Aid Kit

A properly stocked first aid kit is essential to any camping trip. First aid kits can be obtained from camping stores, the Red Cross, or pharmacies. Medical kits can also be homemade from individual items purchased from a pharmacy or supermarket, which is cheaper and sometimes the better approach. Many kits can be bulky, which is all right if there is room in a vehicle, but less practical otherwise. Remember, if travelling far from townships, proper medical attention may be several hours away at least; the function of first aid is to preserve life while minimising complications until such medical help is available. The first aid kit should contain adequate materials to fulfil this function. Campers can carry personal first aid kits, or consolidate materials into one large kit that can be stored in a waterproof container and placed inside a vehicle or tent.

Although some basic first aid treatments are described throughout this chapter, it is advised that all campers have access to, and are cognisant with, the complete first aid techniques as described by organisations such as St John's Ambulance Society or the Red Cross, or have attended a first aid course.

A typical first aid kit should contain the following items:

- sterilised bandages (about 15 metres) of various widths. The most common are 10cm and 15cm, although this can be varied due to their elasticity
- large non-adhesive gauze dressings
- adhesive tape and packets of adhesive strips
- aluminised foil rescue blanket
- soluble aspirin and stronger pain relief tablets
- antiseptic/disinfectant/alcohol
- maximum protection sunscreen
- relieving treatment—for example, solarcaine spray, calamine lotion
- cottonwool
- safety pins
- small scissors
- tweezers

Temperature extremes

Visitors to Australia, especially those who venture inland away from the populated coastal strips, are genuinely surprised at the range of temperatures they can experience over a period as short as one or two days. In the non-summer months, hot days in the interior can be followed by cool to very cold nights. In summer, southerly busters and thunderstorms can often bring welcome but sudden drops in temperature, along with heavy rains, winds, hail and lightning. Without southerly changes, summer temperatures can remain above 40°C for several days in a row—a heatwave. The record for consecutive hot days in Australia remains with Marble Bar, Western Australia, in 1923–24: 161 consecutive days above 37°C.

The unpredictability of weather and temperature conditions makes good planning a necessity. This will involve preparing for all eventualities of heat or cold, trading off the marginal benefit of risk minimisation with its cost in additional encumbrance. Regardless of whether the camping trip is being conducted on foot or by vehicle, a warm and, ideally, windproof and waterproof change of clothes should be packed in case of sudden deterioration of weather conditions. If using a vehicle, there is no excuse for inadequate preparation in this regard. Poor planning, combined with bad camping practices, can lead to cases of hypothermia, heat stroke, sunburn, colds and influenza.

Hypothermia is the lowering of body temperature in key organs and may be signalled by tiredness, slowed reactions, uncontrollable shivering and minor awkwardness of movement. The loss in body heat is caused by prolonged exposure to cold conditions, and is exacerbated by high winds that blow warmth away from the body. Hypothermia is a greater risk when spending time in the water, if consuming too much alcohol that drives blood and heat to the skin, if not eating enough food or drinking enough water during the day, or if engaging in strenuous and fatiguing activity. Smaller, thinner people with no excess fat reserves are potentially more susceptible to hypothermia than others. Severe cases of hypothermia can lead to unconsciousness and death, but prevention is relatively simple. The idea is to keep as dry and warm as possible; wear windproof and waterproof clothes, including hats or beanies; take notice of weather conditions; and eat properly. There is little point in battling fierce, cold winds and rain to make the planned campsite if such action renders members of the party sick. It may be better to seek shelter and rest rather than slavishly following preset plans.

Heat stroke and heat exhaustion are conditions arising from the body being overheated and unable to cool down. Symptoms include cramps, dizziness, headaches, nausea and vomiting. Consistent strenuous activities in temperatures above 30°C are likely to cause overheating and dehydration from losses of body water and salts through sweating. In many parts of Australia, dehydration can occur simply by spending several hours

First aid for hypothermia

Getting out of the cold is a good start, preferably into a tent. If the tent is yet to be pitched, exchange wet clothes for dry, warm clothing first. To restore and maintain internal heat, wrap up in a sleeping bag and/or space blanket and eat plenty of food, including warm, sweet drinks.

Symptoms	Treatment
Shivering	Stop walking immediately
Difficulty in manual movements	Drink hot, sweet liquids
Unusual responses	Eat high-energy foods
Loss of clothing goes unnoticed	Protect against the elements
Stumbling	Re-warm with dry clothes
Slurred speech	
Thought processes impaired	
Intense shivering	Drink very hot fluids
Muscle rigidity	Eat only quickly digested foods such as soups
Stumbling	Get out of wind
Blue skin	Remove wet clothes and cover in sleeping
Drowsiness	bag or space blanket
Slow pulse	Have companions build fire if possible
No response to speech	Skin-to-skin reheat necessary—one naked
No reflexes	heat donor in the same sleeping bag
	Keep victim awake—this is crucial
Erratic heartbeat	Seek professional medical treatment
Respiratory and cardiac failure	
Oedema and haemorrhage in lungs	

walking in the sun. A common result of this is disorientation—it's very easy to take a wrong turn on a walking track, and before you know it, you are lost. The trick here is to keep the body as cool, well-watered and nourished as possible. Mountain streams are refreshingly brisk even in summer, and staying in the shaded parts of a waterway is a good method for keeping cool during the hottest part of the day. Wearing a hat to shade the head and drinking plenty of water to replace lost fluids is also vital. Mixing water with a little salt (a teaspoon) is even better. There are many powdered sports drinks on the market that can be added to water to provide additional minerals and trace elements lost through perspiration. Remember, in extremely hot weather, it may be better to change plans to accommodate the heat rather than battle against it. Take it easy, play cards, read or snooze during the hottest periods, and confine the necessary strenuous activity to early morning or late afternoon.

Keeping out of the sun in the hottest part of the day also reduces the chance of sunburn. Sunburn is caused by overlong exposure to short

First aid for heat exhaustion

Remove excess clothing. Retire to a shady spot. Better still, if there is a shady, cool river or lake nearby, float in it. Otherwise use a wet towel or inner sheet and wrap it around you. Frequent cool drinks with sugars, salt or glucose will help to bring down body temperature and restore natural salts and minerals. Aspirin will help in reducing headaches and fever.

ultraviolet radiation (UV). Repeated exposure to UV radiation may lead to skin cancer and eye cataracts. It is sobering to remember that Australia has the highest rate of skin cancer in the world.

The best approach to preventative care is to generally assume that any unprotected exposure to the sun, especially in the middle of the day, is dangerous. Wear a collared shirt, a wide-brimmed hat and sunglasses through the hottest parts of the day. Use a strong sunscreen for any exposed skin on the face and body, and don't forget the top of your feet if your shoes are off. Don't think for a moment that a layer of cloud will block UV radiation for you. The most severe cases of sunburn occur in overcast conditions, when people think they are safe.

First aid for sunburn

Sunburn can be treated adequately with frequent cool rinsing of the affected area. Keep out of the sun and remove constrictive clothing. Severe sunburn may cause blistering of the skin. These blisters should not be broken, but if they do break on their own, remove any loose skin fragments and apply antibacterial ointment. Then dress with a clean gauze strip. The pain of sunburn can be relieved by taking aspirin or by applying an anaesthetic spray.

Bushfires

Given the generous covering of flammable eucalyptus and bush acacias in many of Australia's wilderness areas, the presence of hot and dry conditions also brings with it the risk of bushfire. When high winds are added to this mix, there is a great potential for bushfires to surge out of control, becoming swirling tornadoes of flame that can easily outspeed a four-wheel-drive vehicle. While fire may be a necessary part of life for many plant species in the bush, it is most definitely not a necessary part of life for the Australian camper.

The best approach in dealing with most hazards is to avoid them, and this is especially true of bushfires. At the planning stage of the trip it is a good idea to check the fire danger status of the area with the national parks authorities, particularly if there have been long hot periods without rain. Keeping an eye on weather conditions once you are in the bush, especially gauging the possibility of thunderstorms after a hot, dry spell, can also prepare for the risk of bushfire. Some camping locations may be closed under extreme fire danger conditions, or total fire bans may be in place, making the lighting of any fire—even a cigarette—illegal. If you are camping in high fire danger conditions, it would be a good idea not to build that large, all-nighter bonfire you had planned. Indeed, any fire could be dangerous. Use a fuel stove, and keep the area around the stove clear of debris to prevent any unplanned spread of flame. Or don't use any cooker at all. Hot conditions are an ideal time to experiment with cold menus.

If there is a bushfire when you are camping, wearing long clothes of wool or cotton is the best protection, or reflective blankets if long clothes are not available. Radiated heat from the flames can best be blocked by finding appropriate shelter, such as a large rock or fallen tree log, a running stream or creek, a section of lush rainforest, a car, or a building. A river can be one of the best forms of shelter. Even if the fire leaps the river, it is safer to be in the water. A large clearing, ravine or gully can also be good shelter if you cannot outdistance or outskirt the fire. If you are on land, keep down low where pockets of cooler air will frequently circulate, stay calm and maintain breathing at a steady, controlled rate. Wait for the front to pass, watching out for falling embers. After the front has passed, wait for the ground to cool before venturing out from your shelter.

Contrary to what many people believe, a car can be a safe refuge in a smaller fire. The petrol tank of a car hardly ever explodes because the heated gas escapes through the vent at the cap. At most, the fire might light the escaping gas and cause a flame to spurt from the cap, but this flame will not run back down into the tank. If you are inside a car when a fire approaches, close the windows and doors, close any ventilation system, duck down low and cover up. Don't panic or think you can escape on foot—you are far safer inside the car than outside, facing the radiant heat. After some time the fire front will pass, the temperature in the car will cool down, and it will be safe to emerge.

Keep assessing the position and strength of the fire, and maintain an escape route plan. Sometimes this may mean passing through the fire front itself. But be careful, this should only be attempted if the flames are not too high (less than 1.5 metres) or too deep, if the area does not contain thick, highly combustible scrub and undergrowth, and if safe ground can be seen clearly on the other side. Keep your skin covered, which includes wearing a cap to protect against falling cinders and ash, and try to pass through the

First aid for burns and scalds

Burns should be cooled by rinsing and immersion in cold water, or by applying wet cloth strips until there is no increase in pain once the cloth is removed. Make sure any burning clothing is extinguished. Do not apply anything to soothe the burn, but cover with dry, sterile dressings. If the burn extends to the fingers or toes, place dressings between them to prevent them from sticking to each other. Infection is a hazard with all burn injuries, so keep the area as sterile as possible. Provide small, cold drinks, preferably with salt, to replenish lost fluids. Burn injuries can also be accompanied by shock. If this happens, have the victim lie down and elevate the legs to increase the flow of blood to vital organs, loosen any restrictive clothing and provide reassurance. Scalds and electrical burns can be treated in the same manner as heat burns.

sides of the fire (across-wind) instead of the direct front (upwind), where the fire will be at its most fierce. Avoid going uphill to escape a bushfire, especially up a cliff. Fires gather intensity and speed travelling uphill, and can easily outpace you. Smoke can indicate which way the wind is driving the fire. Where possible, plan an escape route away from the fire and into any prevailing wind. The fire front will be travelling more slowly on this side, and will also be at its weakest.

Cyclones and high winds

High winds can be a danger in the Australian bush. Winds are caused by the heating of the earth by the sun and the earth's rotation, and can range from the severe tropical cyclones common to northern Australia between November and April, to more gentle coastal sea breezes. Winds can spring up overnight, as the temperature drops, or as new weather systems develop. Cyclonic winds can reach speeds of over 200 km/h, but such systems weaken over land. Still, no camp should be maintained or even attempted if a cyclone warning is issued, for not only do cyclones bring devastating winds, but also torrential flooding rains. Southerly busters are sudden wind squalls which replace hot north-westerly winds near the coast, bringing sudden temperature changes of 10 to 15°C and wind speeds of up to 135 km/h. Winds can also be generated topographically—that is, through the natural features of the landscape, such as mountains, hills and valleys. Downslope winds, such as the Adelaide gully wind on the Mount Lofty Ranges can, under certain conditions, gust up to 185 km/h. The potential for winds should be assessed whenever a camp is set, taking care to avoid camping under trees with dead branches or those that have a reputation for not weathering windy conditions particularly well, such as river red gums.

Thunderstorms and lightning

Be alert to the threat of a thunderstorm. The lightning and thunder can be used to discern how distant the storm is, and repeated tests can reveal how fast it is travelling. Count, in seconds, the time between a lightning flash and its associated thunderclap. Divide this time by three to give the distance from you in kilometres. For example, a six-second gap between the lightning strike and the clap of thunder means that the storm is approximately two kilometres away. This rule of thumb is useful at night, when cumulonimbus clouds are hard to see. Further evidence of lightning and

First aid for falls: broken bones, head and spinal injuries

A broken arm or leg from a fall calls for professional medical care as soon as possible. In some cases the broken bone is evidenced by pain, swelling and deformity around the break; in extreme cases the bone may extrude from the skin. With an open fracture, bleeding should be controlled and the wound covered by a sterile dressing. Immobilise the whole limb with splints or slings cut from straight branches and check that circulation is not impeded.

Head and spinal injuries are much more serious. Head injuries may be evidenced by visible wounds, lapses of consciousness, headaches, vomiting, blurred vision or bleeding from the nose or ears. The symptoms of spinal injuries may include tingling in the hands and feet, loss of movement, deformity of the spine or irregular breathing. Treating head and spinal injuries requires specialist care and medical help should be sought immediately. In the meantime, if the person is unconscious, monitor airways, breathing and circulation. Control any bleeding but avoid direct pressure to the skull. Support the head and neck, and place the person in a side-on recovery position if unconscious, or in the shock position with the legs elevated.

thunder is a short burst of static interrupting a radio broadcast. This can affect an area up to 50 kilometres from the storm.

If a thunderstorm approaches your campsite, make sure all loose equipment is bundled together and tied down, and all tents are secure. If you have a vehicle, keep it parked in a sheltered location. Check that the campsite is not improperly located in or near a dry watercourse. Check the trees near the camp for dead branches, and to determine how they might handle high winds. Lightning will seek the path of least resistance between the earth and the cloud, and this includes people. For this reason, avoid high earth points such as lone trees, boulders, or the tops of hills and ranges during a thunderstorm. Avoid metal structures such as fences, and do not hold metal objects while lightning is present. Keep low and minimise the contact points made by the body with the ground by sitting in a huddled position, knees up to the chin and heels close to the body. If the ground is wet, sit on dry material that will provide insulation, such as rubber-soled shoes, rucksacks and climbing rope. Cave entrances can be a dangerous refuge in an electrical storm as lightning has been known to spark *across* the cave mouth. Move several metres inside the cave, if possible, before setting up camp.

Rivers and waterways

River crossings can be hazardous at any time. If there has been recent heavy rain and the water level has risen, river crossings can become dangerous. If you are heading into territory with large rivers or steep rocky creeks, the basic techniques of river crossing should, ideally, be practiced beforehand. The temptation to keep your feet dry and negotiate waterways by jumping from rock to rock can be risky if the footing is slippery. In many cases, the best way to cross a river or stream is by finding a safe, shallow section and walking or wading from one side to the other. Generally, roped river crossings are discouraged—they should only be used in dire emergencies, if at all—individual and mutual support methods are best.

As with any dangers in the bush, it pays to be cautious. Be wary of:

- fast-moving, unclear water or deep water
- water with flotsam and debris in the current
- unstable or rocking boulders and slippery footing
- underwater snags, such as half-submerged trees or branches
- whirlpools or eddies where the current greets the sides of a bluff
- cold water temperature which can cause hypothermia or shock
- downstream rapids or falls.

Choose an entry point upstream about three or four times the width of the river from your intended exit point downstream on the other side. This will allow the current to aid your progress across the river, rather than forcing a straight crossing.

Wear a pair of sturdy boots in the river to avoid cuts and scratches and to maintain your footing. All material in the packs should be wrapped up in waterproof bags or a groundsheet. Depending on the size and strength of the river, these packs can either be worn or floated across the river, with you wading or swimming behind. This is the best method when the current is relatively slow and the waterway is deep. Most packs float well. For wide rivers, the packs can be linked together by the armstraps to form a makeshift raft.

With a faster current and shallower depth, a mutual support method is recommended for a group crossing. Members of the party should form a line, standing side by side and holding onto each other's clothing or belt straps. Alternatively, the party may hold a long thin pole in front of them, with arms hooked together. The party should cross the river, side on to the

First aid for resuscitation

If you are intending to camp near waterways, rivers, lakes or the coast, it is advisable to know the resuscitation techniques of mouth-to-mouth and heart massage. These techniques can also be useful in treating injuries such as snakebite, electrical shock or heart attack. A basic approach is described here, but reference to a specialised first aid text or, preferably, a first aid course is recommended.

A person in danger of drowning may experience heart or breathing failure and require immediate resuscitation. Place the victim on his side with his face downwards, clear any obstruction to the airways, and allow mucus or water to drain from the mouth. Then roll him on his back and, with his head tilted back, commence resuscitation procedures.

Pinch the nostrils closed, open your mouth over the victim's mouth and blow strongly. The victim's chest should rise—if not, there is a blockage in the airway. After this first breath, expel five quick breaths through your mouth and check for pulse in the neck. If there is a pulse beat, keep applying mouth-to-mouth respiration at 12 breaths per minute. If there is no pulse, then commence heart massage. Press down about five centimetres on the lower half of the breastbone with the heel of your hand. This should be done at least once per second. If you are working alone with the victim, alternate 15 chest presses to two lung inflations. If there are two people, alternate five chest presses with one lung inflation. Once breathing recommences, roll the victim onto his side, as vomiting will invariably occur.

current, with the strongest person at the upstream position, where the river current is most forceful. This is a relatively safe method.

When crossing a river alone, use a pole or branch about two metres long as a prop. Moving across the river, place the pole across your body and upstream from your feet, using the pole as a 'third leg'. Step cautiously to avoid snags and holes.

Coastal waters

People are fascinated by the sea, and with over 35 000 kilometres of mainland coastline to explore, camping by the sea is a very popular summer activity in Australia. There are many hazards to coastal camping to be aware of: the enhanced danger of sunburn and overexposure, infections from coral cuts or stingers, the dangerous marine animals (see page 61), as well as the risks of drowning. If you are unlucky enough to get caught in a rip—distinguishable by the water being either choppier, darker, or, in some cases, noticeably calmer—the best action to take is to let the rip carry you out until its strength dissipates. Then swim parallel to the shore for about 30 metres before coming back in. Avoid swimming in the surf directly after eating, as cramps may occur when bloodflow is diverted to the digestive system, and never swim after consuming alcohol.

Desert and semi-arid terrain

Being one of the driest continents on earth presents special risks, especially when camping in the arid or semi-arid regions across the centre of Australia. While this area isn't all desert, it shares the similar traits of low average rainfall, sparse vegetation, temperature extremes and clear, wide skies. The countryside is very flat and potentially monotonous, but there are also some fascinating ranges in the Pilbara, the Flinders and in the Centre to pique the interest of campers and those looking for the ultimate sunset photograph. Maintaining an adequate water supply is the chief concern in these parts. We can survive for as long as a few weeks without food, but without water the survival period shrinks to a few days. The body needs 2–10 litres of water per day, depending on temperature and individual body metabolism. Keep reserves full in tanks in the vehicle, bring foods with high water content such as fruit and vegetables, and take note of re-supply points on the map. Low water supplies can become polluted, so it pays to pack water purifiers as an additional precaution. On very hot days, keep activity to a minimum to prevent dehydration. The best time to visit the Centre is in winter, when the heat is less fierce.

Although it doesn't rain very often in semi-arid areas, when it does it comes down by the bucketful. Dusty tracks and trails can become boggy very quickly, and access can be cut for days. Because of the parched earth, rain can run off briskly, flowing into dry creek beds. For this reason, choose campsites that will be free from any run-off.

Cliffs and rocks

The rugged cliff tops, gorges and gullies that characterise Australia's mountain ranges, coastlines and outback regions offer some of the most breathtaking natural vistas in the world—a vision splendid for the camper or wilderness enthusiast. With a little common sense, rocks and cliff falls are easy to avoid.

Most people experience a sense of vertigo as they approach a cliff top and for this reason it is best to keep as close to the ground as possible when nearing the edge. If the urge to look over the edge is simply too great to resist, then do it by lying down flat and keeping your stomach on the ground. Many cliffs along the Great Dividing Range are made from sedimentary rocks such as sandstone, which crumble and shear from the effects of winds and rain. When walking at the base of a cliff, be wary of falling rocks, and try to avoid dislodging rocks and material if negotiating a cliff or walking along the top. Consult specialist guidebooks for proper instructions of abseiling and rock climbing. See pages 80-83 for introductory techniques.

Dangerous animals and plants

Snakes and spiders

Snakes and spiders are the two deadliest land creatures in Australia, yet bites from snakes and spiders in the bush are rare, and fatalities from bites much rarer still. Of the many species of Australian spiders, only two are known to be highly venomous: the Sydney funnel-web spider, which is more likely to be found in the suburbs of Sydney than in your tent, and the red-back spider. Many spiders look big, hairy and threatening, but their appearance is often far more troublesome than the actual effects of their bite.

Of the 190 recognised species of Australian snakes, approximately 22 are at least as deadly as the Asian cobra. The timid inland taipan has a well-deserved reputation as the most venomous snake in the world, having 50 times the toxicity of the cobra. The eastern brown, with its aggressive behaviour, is second in the rankings.

A little reading and research will help you to identify snakes and spiders found in the bush and allay any irrational fears. These creatures have more to fear from campers than the other way around, and will retreat if caught out in the open. As with most hazards when camping, prevention is the key. The following steps are useful in avoiding snake and spider bites:

- wear solid footwear (boots) even gaiters for long pants if in snake country
- be careful placing your hands or feet in any hollows or cracks
- keep the fly of your tent zipped up to prevent entry of any uninvited guests
- keep your shoes inside the tent
- inspect your shoes and sleeping bag before use
- walk heavily
- carry a torch at night.

First aid for snake, spider and scorpion bites

Only a small proportion of snake species are venomous, and the majority of bites are treatable. Keep the injured person still and calm. This not only keeps up the spirits, but also reduces the heart rate and flow of any poison around the body. Apply pressure directly to the bite. Tightly bandage the limb from the top down, ensure the limb is kept lower than the heart and treat the person for shock if necessary. Transport the injured person to a hospital or doctor as soon as possible. Do not wash the bite, as traces of venom on the skin can help in identifying the snake involved. This first aid approach is also the correct one for funnel-web spider bites, and scorpion and blue-ringed octopus stings.

Crocodiles

There are two main species of crocodile in Australia: the very aggressive estuarine crocodile, which grows 3–5 metres in length, and the relatively harmless 2–3 metre freshwater crocodile. Both species inhabit the tropical north of the continent, occupying the coastal and nearby inland areas from Western Australia, the Northern Territory and Queensland. They mainly feed on fish, mammals, birds and crustaceans. The estuarine crocodile lives in coastal rivers and swamps and may occasionally be found in the open sea; the freshwater crocodile is usually located in rivers and billabongs. Crocodiles are a protected species and are becoming more numerous and larger. They are one of the few animals in Australia capable of eating people, along with sharks. If you are camping in crocodile country:

- do not swim in low-lying rivers and waterways, and take care in higher streams
- do not camp beside a large body of water, but stay well inland
- stay alert when near the edges of waterways, or in small boats or canoes.

Sharks and other marine animals

Shark attacks are rare in Australia, but it is wise to check for any reported sightings. People have a somewhat irrational fear of sharks, and in many cases that dorsal fin sighted in the ocean will more likely belong to a curious, friendly dolphin. The presence of dolphins is actually a good sign, given their animosity towards sharks feeding in their waters. Sharks usually feed in the ocean's depths and, given the abundance of fish and other marine animals in tropical waters, are unlikely to seek food nearer to the surface. However, a hungry shark may follow fish to the surface. Sharks in this mood are likely to be dangerous and, if sighted, should be avoided. Still, it is worth remembering that many more people die from drowning in Australia's surf each year than are attacked by sharks.

Sharks are not the only lethal marine threat, however. On Australia's coasts can be found other, potentially lethal animals such as the venomous blue-ringed octopus; the stonefish, which injects poison through its sharp dorsal spines when trodden upon; the box jellyfish; and varieties of stinging shellfish. Of these, the box jellyfish causes more deaths than sharks, crocodiles, stonefish and other marine animals combined. Wearing sturdy footwear and staying alert are the best ways to avoid stonefish and shellfish stings. Box jellyfish may be found anywhere on the coasts north of the Tropic of Capricorn, especially in summer and early autumn.

First aid for box jellyfish sting

The venom of the box jellyfish may have three distinct effects. Primarily, it can stop breathing and heartbeat causing death in minutes. It can also kill red blood cells and destroy skin tissue. Venom is injected through the tentacles, which can reach up to 3 metres in length. An immediate call should be made for antivenom, which is often held by hospitals, doctors and lifesaving clubs along tropical coasts, and in some shops and private homes in remote areas. Apply vinegar to the welts to deactivate undischarged venom cells. Be prepared to apply resuscitation techniques. Do not move the victim until normal breathing has been restored for at least 10 minutes, nor try to remove any remaining tentacles because they will discharge more venom.

Over 30 species of sea snakes are found in tropical Australian waters, and their venom is toxic enough to cause death by muscle destruction. More irritating and painful than deadly are the bluebottles and other marine stingers that float in the tides of tropical waters during summer, closing many beaches for swimmers.

Feral pigs, wild dogs and dingoes

While recorded attacks from feral pigs are few in number, it is best to keep clear of these animals if spotted. Licensed gun-owners and professional hunters track and destroy feral pig populations that become a nuisance to nearby farms. Packs of wild dogs are extremely rare but can be quite dangerous—certainly more dangerous than a dingo. The much-maligned dingo is mainly a scavenger and hunter of small prey; unless starved or disturbed, it will hardly ever directly attack people. Dingoes can be very inquisitive, however, and it is best to dispose of any food scraps wisely rather than leaving them lying around a campsite or inside a tent.

Bush bloodsuckers

Apart from the more dangerous creatures of Australia's wilderness and coasts, there is also quite a large range of insects, parasites and small animals that, while certainly not life-threatening for bushwalkers and campers, can be a real nuisance.

Ticks are eight-legged parasites that attach themselves to the skin of mammals, birds and reptiles to suck their blood. Small children and animals, as well as people who are allergic to the tick's secretions into the bloodstream, may be more affected. A tick is best removed by gripping it firmly with tweezers at the point of attachment to the skin, turning it onto its back, and pulling. Try not to leave the head buried in the skin, as this could cause prolonged irritation.

First aid for leeches

There are several ways to encourage a leech to detach itself from the skin: a lighted match, a dab of salt or a drop of methylated spirits will do the trick. It is likely that there will be a lot of bleeding, but this can be stopped by applying an adhesive strip. To remove a leech from the eye, dab the free end of the leech with a moist handkerchief or cloth dipped in salt.

Leeches also feed on the blood of other animals, their tiny razor-sharp 'teeth' and anticoagulant secretions maintaining a steady blood flow into the worm-like body. Leeches are found in moist, warm and wet areas, near creeks and in rainforest. Frequent applications of insect repellent and the wearing of sturdy shoes and gaiters— even strong stockings under your socks—can help in avoiding leeches, which mainly attach themselves to the lower legs and feet. Otherwise, the blood-soaked sock is usually the first sign of their presence. Leeches are harmless, despite the quantity of bleeding they cause. The only real concern lies in any infection that might set in if the wound is left untreated.

Mosquitoes are the bane of the bush. While in most situations harmless, in certain country and tropical areas mosquitoes are known to carry the debilitating virus Ross River fever, and dengue fever in the tropics. Furthermore, pockets of malaria may still be found in remote parts of the north coast. Mosquito bites are a nuisance for the itching and scratching they cause. Insect repellent, clothing made of tightly-woven material, smoky campfires, and mosquito-proof nets on tents are the best defences against mosquitoes.

Bush stingers

Many Australian creatures can deliver a painful sting, or worse. Examples include scorpions, bull ants, soldier ants, wasps, sandflies, centipedes and non-indigenous bee species. Avoiding these stingers is best achieved by being alert to their potential presence, using repellents where necessary, and by checking footwear and sleeping bags before use.

First aid for stings

A bee or wasp sting that is still lodged in the skin can be removed with tweezers or scratched out with a clean fingernail. In rare circumstances the injured person may feel weak, faint or have difficulty in breathing, so be prepared to apply resuscitation techniques if necessary. A cold compress will reduce swelling, and any itching and pain can be relieved with calamine lotion.

Dangerous plants

Some plants can cause problems for unsuspecting children or adults, or amateur botanists who want to taste unfamiliar roots, leaves, nuts or fruits. Many plants are poisonous to eat—especially the many species of fungi—or may be poisonous by inhalation or by contact with the skin or the eyes. Direct contact with the giant stinging tree or nettles may constitute dermal poisoning, causing skin blisters, rashes or irritating itches. Burning plants with toxicity in the roots, stems, leaves or flowers may also poison through inhalation of the resulting toxic fumes. In spring, the abundance of pollinating plants in the bush could cause major problems for people with allergies or asthmatic conditions.

Water quality

While many remote streams may be safe, it is best to check water quality first before drinking, since even clear water can harbour nasty micro-organisms. Some streams look dirty, but this may simply be due to floating clay particles or the naturally occurring, common and harmless 'tea-tree staining' from tannic acids in nearby vegetation. Of greater concern are the highly toxic blue-green algae blooms in low-flowing streams high in nutrients and exposed to strong sunlight. Natural watercourses may also contain bacteria, viruses and protozoa such as *Cryptosporidium* and *Giardia*, which are all derived from exposed human and other animal faecal matter. Imbibing some of these bugs can cause severe gastroenteritis, the symptoms being many days of vomiting and diarrhoea. Some of the most affected areas in Australia are the alpine regions.

Methods of neutralisation

1 Boiling

Boiling will kill all micro-organisms within a few minutes and is one of the simplest and most effective ways to purify water. Unfortunately, it uses a lot of fuel in the process—which may have to be carried into camp. This may be the best option if there is a lot of fuel available, or if little bush-walking or hiking is required.

Boiling contaminated water for one minute is adequate to kill *Giardia* as well as most other bacterial or viral pathogens that are likely to be acquired from drinking polluted water. However, you should keep in mind that at higher altitudes, water is likely to boil at colder temperatures. *Giardia* becomes completely inactivated when heated to 70°C for 10 minutes. Heating to 50–60°C for 10 minutes produces only approximately 95–98 per cent inactivation, respectively.

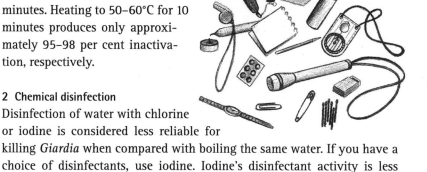

2 Chemical disinfection
Disinfection of water with chlorine or iodine is considered less reliable for killing *Giardia* when compared with boiling the same water. If you have a choice of disinfectants, use iodine. Iodine's disinfectant activity is less likely than chlorine to be reduced by unfavourable water conditions—such as dissolved organic material in water—or by water with a high pH value.

3 Water filters
There is a wide range of water filters and purifiers on the market that can reduce the risks associated with poor water quality. For example, to remove *Giardia* cysts, a water filter must have sufficiently small pores to trap the cysts and a large enough capacity to produce a useful volume of treated water before backwashing or replacement is necessary. Filters and purifiers can be expensive and time-consuming, but they clean water well and are lighter in weight than the equivalent fuel required to boil water.

A warning about iodine

Iodine is a component of the thyroid hormone thyroxin that helps to regulate our growth, development and metabolic rate. Excessive intakes of iodine can cause enlargement of the thyroid gland and depressed thyroid activity. For *Giardia* control, or if the water is cold or of poor quality, directions on packets of tablets usually recommend using extra high doses. The average backpacker will drink several litres a day, so the continued use of iodine tablets is not recommended.

Cooking: How to prepare camp food (that'll stay down)

In many ways, cooking and eating a hearty campfire dinner at the end of a day's walking is one of the most enjoyable aspects of camping. With a little planning and imagination there is no reason why eating in the bush cannot be the stellar experience to match the nightly light show in the heavens above. Certainly, for campers on the move, weight and encumbrance factors, as well as the general nutritional value issues, must be carefully considered. One of the greatest dilemmas to be tackled by the budding or experienced camp chef is how to choose between the huge variety of foods that are available. Deciding on the right balance depends on:

- personal likes and dislikes
- nutritional value
- weight and space limitations
- the length of the trip
- the weather conditions expected
- the camping facilities available
- including a variety of foods.

Nutrition

Everybody needs energy, even the blissfully inactive campers who prefer to snooze their way through the day. The body needs energy to think, to breathe and circulate blood, to repair muscles and tissues, to maintain body fats. The energy we get from the foods we eat is measured as calories or kilojoules. Most nutritionists today use kilojoules as the standard unit of measurement, one calorie being equal to roughly 4.2 kilojoules. Generally speaking, the body requires about 8000 kilojoules a day, even during inactive periods. When walking along a track or pottering around a campsite, this figure will rise to something like 15 000 kilojoules a day, or even more than 20 000 kilojoules a day in very cold conditions. Engaging in extreme, high-octane bush sports may require between 30 000–40 000 kilojoules for the day's exertions.

Most foods contain proteins, carbohydrates and fats. These three groups all provide energy, but work in different ways. Carbohydrates are an immediate energy source; a welcome booster when engaged in vigorous outdoor activities. Foods with a high carbohydrate content include sweets, sugar, honey, rice, pasta, bread and dried fruit. Proteins assist in the daily repair of muscles and tissue. High protein foods include lean meat, eggs, milk, cheese, fish and beans. Fats are essential if contemplating heavy activity in cool conditions because they contain the highest energy per gram consumed, but is much more slowly digested than carbohydrates and proteins, requiring an adequate intake of water. Butter, meat fat, bacon, chocolate, nuts and full cream milk or milk powder are very good sources of fat and fatty acids.

Ideally, a camp menu would contain foods from all three energy groups. If little strenuous activity is planned, the ratio of carbohydrates to proteins and fats should be approximately 4:1:1. The more activities planned, the higher should be the fat content, towards 3:1:2. Given these ideal ratios of carbohydrates to proteins to fats, and making allowances for the addition of water and other non-energy food components, the moderately active, average camper will require roughly one kilogram of food to maintain body mass. If venturing into colder climes, or planning a more physical trip, more food will be required.

Out of the three food groups, proteins are usually the most difficult to maintain in a well-balanced camp diet, especially when contemplating a basic vegetarian diet. Red meat is one of the best sources of protein, but it is generally hard to keep or carry over long distances. The solution is to use a variety of high-protein vegetable foods in the diet, such as combining beans with rice or seeds (sunflower or pumpkin), thereby minimising the quantity of meat to be carried.

Drinks

Water is essential for the human body and we need 2–10 litres of pure water a day, depending on the temperature and the level of activity. Water is usually the only ingredient we can expect to find an adequate supply of in the bush—not only for liquid refreshment but also for rehydrating dried foods for eating—and so it is important to plan for a campsite which has ready access to water.

Mixing isotonic sports drink powders with water can also replenish energy and provide additional minerals and trace elements. The length of a typical camping trip usually rules out the possibility of suffering severe vitamin deficiencies, especially when the rest of the diet is good, but if you are camping for a couple of weeks or more, consideration should be given to supplementing the diet with vitamin pills—especially from the water-soluble C and B group—or preferably a multivitamin. Salts are lost very regularly, however, and can be a concern if the diet is inadequate. In fact, salt levels can be easily maintained by adding a pinch of table salt to drinking water, or adding salt to meals.

Other popular beverages in camp include tea, coffee, chocolate drinks, fruit juices and powdered fruit drinks. Camping does not mean giving up a great cup of coffee—camping stores sell several ingenious devices that can brew coffee from the smallest campfire or fuel stove. For those with the space, inclination and temperament, a small amount of spirits or a bottle of wine makes an excellent accompaniment to a campfire dinner, or as a mellow after-dinner drink to complement an evening's star-gazing.

Planning a menu

A day's food requirements can be broken down into the three main meals of breakfast, lunch and dinner, and then there are snacks. Breakfast is probably the most important meal of the day, and time should be made to eat well in the morning to get the energy boost for the day. Carbohydrates from porridge or muesli with milk and sugar, stewed fruits and a hot drink are an ideal start. A second course of fats from bacon, eggs and sausages, as well as peanut butter with bread and butter or margarine, provides a longer-term energy store.

Lunch can be varied, depending on the activities planned. If you are walking or engaged in other strenuous activity during the day, time may be short for a large meal. In this case, high-energy biscuits, available from camping shops, are ideal, as are peanut butter and jam sand-wiches, cheeses, dried fruits, muesli bars and cold meats. On short trips, the relative luxuries of cake and fresh fruit provide a welcome energy boost. If settled in camp, lunch can be a more laid-back, scrumptious affair, with fruits, breads, cakes and desserts being added to the mix.

Dinner is the main meal of the day, and it should be varied from day to day, even if cycling through a set three- or four-day menu. Protein-rich foods containing some fat are beneficial for dinner as they help the body to effect repairs and restore body fats during sleep. Soups, vegetables, and a high-protein meal such as steak, followed by desserts of stewed fruit, custards and puddings make excellent, hearty dinners. There is a wide variety of meals that can be prepared for dinner: pastas, fish, rice dishes, noodles, wok dishes with stir-fried strips of meat and vegetables and oriental herbs and spices. The list is as endless as your imagination. Experimentation is the order of the day, and anything left uneaten can be included in breakfast the following morning.

Snacks provide a welcome boost of energy. Foods here typically include chocolate, muesli bars, glucose-rich sweets, nuts, dried fruit and that familiar camping treat-of-sorts, scroggin, achieved by mixing all these foods together in parcels and coating in glucose or brown sugar.

Following a menu such as this will produce something in the order of 15 000–18 000 kilojoules of energy—easily enough for a fairly arduous camping adventure—and will entail carrying a little over one kilogram of food per person per day. When making up a shopping list based on your planned menu, it is best to err on the side of including too much food rather than too little, to allow for any unforeseen developments, delays or emergencies. For similar reasons, it is also smart to include a good proportion of foods that do not require any cooking at all to eat, such as those from the snack list.

Lightweight pre-packaged meals

On those extended camping trips where weight and fuel efficiency is a major concern, dried pre-packaged foods may come in handy. The following information represents a sample of lightweight dinners available from the major manufacturers. See also the tables on pages 76–77.

The process of freeze-drying foods involves removing the ice from frozen foods in a stable, vacuum environment and is considered to reduce the food value only slightly. Rehydrating freeze-dried foods takes only a couple of minutes as the food is extremely porous. Dehydrated foods, on the other hand, are dried by a heating and air-drying process which requires longer rehydration and cooking times. They are not as good if cooking fuel is scarce.

Remember that when using packet dinners or pre-packaged meals, the serving portions are usually small, so pack more than seems necessary. While a little expensive, pre-packaged freeze-dried foods can save time and trouble when camping, and are generally efficient on fuel to cook. This makes them excellent for long treks in the wilderness, where you have to carry fuel, or if there is little fuel available. Packaged meals can be a bit plain and boring, however, so try spicing them up a bit with exotic herbs, or adding fresh vegetables.

Packing and carrying food

After you have made a food list and bought all the ingredients from the supermarket, it is time to start loading the food into packs, rucksacks or in boxes for the vehicle. Regardless of whether you are camping with the vehicle or bushwalking, take the time now to dispose of any unnecessary packaging. Packing food in a rucksack for easy access is an acquired skill that many campers develop through trial and error. Avoid using paper bags and heavy jars or bottles, but use light double plastic or cloth bags, tied with string, twisters or rubber bands instead. Sugar, butter, salt and coffee can be packed in plastic screw-top containers, while jams and other spreads can be tipped into plastic, refillable tubes. Plastic film canisters are useful for storing powders, herbs and spices. Some meals, such as home-prepared delicacies, may be stored in ziplock plastic bags, which lock in the freshness and take up less room in a rucksack.

Cooking and cooking utensils

The following list contains probably as many cooking utensils as anyone should need on a camp, and on most occasions we require even fewer:

- frying pan or mess kit
- cooking pot or billies with lids
- bowls (one per person)
- drinking/measuring cup
- pocket knife/spoon/knife/fork
- wooden stirring spoon
- long-handled spoon/ladle
- billy clamp/tongs
- small spatula
- small can-opener
- camp stove and fuel
- matches
- biodegradable soap
- pot scrubber
- assorted plastic bags, containers and bottles
- aluminium foil.

For most camping trips, the weight of the cooking equipment should be no heavier than 2–3 kilograms. Aluminium is the favoured material for cooking equipment because it is lightweight and an excellent conductor of heat. Stainless steel billies can, however, double as handy mirrors for personal grooming and are generally more durable than aluminium.

While there are many ways to cook in camp, from barbecues and dutch ovens to using various pots and frying pans, the most commonly used cooking utensil is the humble billy. Many meals can be made by simply adding more and more ingredients to whatever is cooking in the pot. Billies come in various shapes and sizes and range in volume from 1.5–4 litres. Although a group of three or four people can get by on a single billy, it is a good idea to pack an extra, smaller billy inside a larger one. This allows for simultaneous cooking or cooking and cleaning, or for brewing tea or coffee while the meal bubbles away. When cooking with a billy, keep the lid on firmly to save time and use less fuel, as well as to prevent insects becoming part of the recipe. Use taller billies for hanging over a fire and squat billies for cooking or boiling on a flat plate. Billies can also be used as primitive ovens by placing the can inside the hot coals of a fire and covering the top with a flat plate and ashes. This oven is good for producing that quintessential Australian bread—damper. The billy really is the all-rounder of the cookery set.

Using stoves

Stoves are a more environmentally friendly approach to camping and cooking than lighting fires. Ensure that you know how the stove works and its safety requirements before trekking out. Make sure there is adequate ventilation when using the stove, and never light a stove inside a tent. Indeed, it is best to keep most hot cooking implements out of tents: they may not set it alight, but they can melt through or scald the material. When cooking with a billy over a stove, ensure that the stove is stable, that no flammable objects are nearby, and that others know that your stove is alight. Furthermore, be aware of how to deal with real-life 'pressure-cooker' situations, such as when your cooking equipment catches alight! Stoves that burn methylated spirits can be safely doused in water; pressurised stoves that use kerosene or shellite cannot be dealt with in this way. Flames extruding from the safety valve of these cookers should be blown out if at all possible, or the stove should be smothered. Failing that, remove the stove to a safe place quickly, and with great care.

Cooking over a fire or a gas stove can never be as easy as cooking at home but it shouldn't be too difficult either, nor an arduous bore. Watching other experienced outdoor chefs and practicing cooking meals at home before setting out will improve your skills and make the whole experience a lot more fun too.

Common camp foods and their energy/nutritional value per 100 grams

Food Item	Energy (kj)	Protein (g)	Fat	Carbo-hydrates (g)	Dietary Fibre (g)	Cholest-erol (mg)
Apple (raw)	230	0.3	tr	13.8	2.1	0
Apricot (dried)	819	4.3	0.2	44.4	9.1	0
Apricot (raw)	156	0.8	0.1	7.4	2.1	0
Bacon, breakfast (fried)	637	21.9	5.8	3.1	0	53
Banana (raw)	358	1.7	0.1	19.9	2.2	0
Barley, pearl (boiled)	445	3.1	0.9	21.1	3.5	0
Barley, pearl (raw)	1270	8.6	2.4	61.2	9.7	0
Bean, soya (dried)	1420	31.3	20.2	7.4	20.1	0
Biscuit (Anzac)	1930	6.2	24.1	56.9	3.6	18
Biscuit (chocolate)	1830	6.2	17.2	65.3	1.9	15
Bran, oat (raw)	1030	17.3	7.0	50.3	15.9	0
Bread (brown)	968	9.7	2.5	41.9	5.0	0
Bread (white regular)	1040	8.6	2.5	47.3	2.7	0
Bread (wholemeal)	939	10.1	2.9	38.9	6.5	0
Butter, regular	3040	0.8	81.4	1.0	0	200
Cheese (cheddar)	1690	25.4	33.8	0.1	0	101
Cheese (parmesan)	1850	38.1	32.4	0.1	0	95
Chocolate, milk	2160	8.6	27.4	62.0	0.8	18
Coffee powder	424	13.6	0.6	10.1	16.4	tr
Cracker, water	1710	9.9	9.3	71.0	2.8	3
Crispbread, rye	1340	10.8	2.5	62.6	14.3	tr
Crumpet	779	5.1	0.7	39.2	2.3	tr
Custard powder	400	0.4	0.2	27.0	na	111
Date (dried)	1130	2.0	0.2	67.2	9.7	0

NOTE: tr = trace elements detected, na = not available

Common Camp Foods and their Energy/Nutritional Value per 100 grams

Food Item	Energy (kJ)	Protein (g)	Fat (g)	Carbo-hydrates (g)	Dietary Fibre (g)	Choles-terol (mg)
Egg (hardboiled)	632	13.2	10.9	0.3	0	429
Egg (raw)	594	12.7	10.1	0.3	0	375
Frankfurter (simmered)	1040	14.3	19.9	3.4	1.8	58
Fruit, mixed (dried)	1120	2.0	0.9	65.2	5.6	0
Honey	1320	0.3	0	82.1	0	0
Jam, berry	1090	0.3	0	67.3	1.6	0
Lentil (dried)	1090	24.2	2.0	35.0	13.7	0
Mandarin	168	1.0	0.2	8.1	2.2	0
Margarine	2990	0.4	80.5	0.6	0	0
Meat, beef (fillet steak)	821	30.2	8.3	0	0	82
Meat, mince	902	26.7	12.1	0	0	93
Milk powder, skim	1470	36.2	1.0	51.3	0	32
Milk powder, whole	2030	26.9	26.2	37.7	0	100
Milk, skim	145	3.5	0.1	5.0	0	4
Milk, whole	271	3.4	3.8	4.6	0	14
Milo (chocolate powder)	1570	12.6	10.5	59.8	0	28
Muesli bar, fruit	1550	4.8	14.8	55.8	3.9	tr
Muesli, toasted	1690	9.2	16.6	55.0	8.7	0
Muffin, English	836	9.8	1.4	36.5	2.4	tr
Oats, rolled (raw)	1550	10.7	8.5	61.8	6.9	0
Oil, canola	3700	0	100.0	0	0	0
Onion, raw	112	1.7	0.2	4.6	2.2	0
Orange	160	1.1	0.1	8.1	2.0	0
Pasta, egg (boiled)	547	5.3	0.6	25.6	1.0	0
Pasta, egg (dry)	1470	12.8	1.5	70.2	2.6	18
Pea, dried	194	5.0	0.3	5.9	4.9	0

NOTE: tr = trace elements detected, na = not available

Common Camp Foods and their Energy/Nutritional Value per 100 grams

Food Item	Energy (kJ)	Protein (g)	Fat (g)	Carbo-hydrates (g)	Dietary Fibre (g)	Choles-terol (mg)
Pea, regular	249	5.8	0.4	8.1	5.6	0
Peanut butter	2510	27.7	51.6	8.1	10.9	0
Potato, raw	447	3.0	2.8	17.2	1.5	0
Prune	778	2.3	0.4	43.9	7.8	0
Rice, white (boiled)	630	2.3	0.2	28.0	0.8	0
Rice, white (raw)	1470	6.6	0.5	79.1	2.3	0
Salmon, pink (canned)	545	19.4	5.8	0	0	69
Salmon, red (canned)	815	21.9	12.0	0	0	71
Sardine (canned in oil)	1280	17.6	26.6	0	0	122
Soup powder (35 g)	794	3.8	6.9	27.8	na	0
Spam (canned)	1380	12.5	31.0	1.3	0.5	
Spirits (100 mls)	852	0	0	0.1	0	0
Sports powder (100 mls)	121	0	0	6.7	0	0
Sugar, white	1600	0	0	100	0	0
Sultana	1280	2.8	0.4	75.0	4.4	0
Tuna (canned in brine)	458	22.1	2.2	0	0	43
Tuna (canned in oil)	1210	20.8	23.2	0	0	33
Vegemite	589	24.4	1.0	8.1	0	0
Wine, red (100 mls)	283	0.2	0	0	0	0

NOTE: tr = trace elements detected, na = not available

Source: English, R. and J. Lewis (1991) *Nutritional Values of Australian Foods*, AGPS.

Pre-packaged meals

Manufacturer / Product	Drying Process	Dry weight	Energy per serve	Carbohydrates per serve	Protein per serve	Fats per serve	Serves
AlpineAire (New Zealand)							
Cheese nut casserole	Freeze / dehydrated	184g	1557kJ	62g	16g	16g	2
Leonardo da fettuccine	Freeze / dehydrated	155g	1235kJ	45g	15g	3g	2
Pasta Roma	Dehydrated	170g	1373kJ	47g	18g	1g	2
Spaghetti in mushroom sauce	Dehydrated	155g	1076kJ	50g	18g	1g	2
Shrimp Newburg	Freeze / dehydrated	170g	1331kJ	49g	16g	6g	2
Santa Fe black bean and rice	Freeze / dehydrated	184g	1370kJ	69g	10g	2g	2
Albacore tuna with noodles and cheese	Freeze-dried	155g	1360kJ	39g	23g	7g	2
Backpackers Pantry (USA)							
Vegetable stew	Freeze-dried	99g	N/A	N/A	N/A	N/A	2
Spaghetti and sauce	Freeze-dried	202g	N/A	N/A	N/A	N/A	2
Chilli and beans	Freeze-dried	198g	1633kJ	48g	28g	18g	2
Bombay lentil curry	Freeze-dried	220g	N/A	N/A	N/A	N/A	2
No-cook lasagne	Freeze-dried	198g	N/A	N/A	N/A	N/A	2
Chilli-cheese Nachos	Freeze-dried	255g	N/A	N/A	N/A	N/A	2

Pre-packaged meals

Manufacturer / Product	Drying Process	Dry weight	Energy per serve	Carbohydrates per serve	Protein per serve	Fats per serve	Serves
Harvest Foodworks (CANADA)							
Alfredo Primavera	Freeze / dehydrated	216g	1900kJ	58g	19g	17g	2
Bountiful pasta	Freeze / dehydrated	247g	2014kJ	82g	17g	9g	2
Chilli Mexicana	Freeze / dehydrated	219g	1532kJ	68g	22g	3g	2
Garden vegetable stew	Freeze / dehydrated	216g	1549kJ	75g	16g	2g	2
Mediterranean pasta delight	Freeze / dehydrated	237g	1658kJ	73g	27g	2g	2
Stroganoff	Freeze / dehydrated	246g	1863kJ	72g	25g	8g	2
Adventure Foods (AUS)							
Chicken tetrazzini	Freeze-dried	110g	2070kJ	52g	28g	21g	2
Hearty beef and beans	Freeze-dried	75g	1540kJ	9g	40g	19g	2
Spaghetti bolognaise	Freeze-dried	110g	2210kJ	46g	35g	24g	2

Source: Wild Magazine (No. 52) & store surveys

N/A – Not applicable

Note: Products listed are available from good camping stores in Australia.

DIY drying

An alternative to purchasing dried foods is to dry the food at home yourself. Many foods, fruits and vegetables especially, are 70–90 per cent water. Dried foods pack in a lot more energy per unit weight and can be easily rehydrated once in camp. Some dried foods taste great dried and do not need rehydrating. One of the simplest and least expensive ways to get into home drying is to use a food dryer that comes with a heating element, trays and fan. Many foods can be dried in this way, including vegetables, fruits and meats. Vegetables should be peeled and cut into thin strips. Fruit can be sliced and dried, then coated in honey or salt for a high-energy snack. Alternatively, the home oven can be used for drying, but use a low heat and keep the door open to prevent the food from being cooked instead of dried.

Bush foods

In recent times, interest in traditional Australian bush foods has escalated, although eating native flora and fauna is illegal in all national parks—something to consider unless the issue is one of immediate survival. Nutritionally, bush foods based on fruits, seeds, nuts and berries are higher in complex carbohydrates and dietary fibre than non-native equivalents. Wattle species have edible seeds, gums and roots that are high in protein, complex carbohydrates and fibre. Yams refer to the underground tubers of the vine species *Dioscorea*, which, when cooked, taste a little like sweet potato. Yams are eaten with shellfish or finfish in northern Australia, providing a rich source of starchy carbohydrates. Bogong moths are almost as well-known in Australia as witjuti (witchetty) grubs, and many invade cities along the east coast of New South Wales and inland as they migrate from the warmer climes of southern Queensland to the Bogong Mountains on the Victorian border. Here the moths shelter in massive numbers under granite creches; a veritable feast with the taste of snow gum nectar, and one which is high in proteins and essential fats for anyone willing to try, either heated up or eaten raw.

There are many other bush foods available to the hungry camper or bushwalker: lilies, figs, tamarinds, pigweed seeds, boab fruits, native grapes, the nectars of various species of grevilleas, banksias and waratahs. Research is recommended before preparing and eating any bush food. Some are poisonous unless prepared correctly. Sufficient knowledge in this field can be a rewarding experience, opening a window onto traditional Aboriginal culture and giving you the chance to eat real bush tucker.

Activities: All fun and games until you're up the creek

People venture into the bush for many reasons. Some just want a relaxing escape from the rat-race, others want to spend some quality time with their family and friends. Some go for inspiration, others seek to achieve personal goals and challenges. Still others can be described simply as death-wishers looking for a thrill. We have come a long way from the days when the bush was viewed as an uninteresting wasteland—there is so much to do in the bush and so little time.

BUSH SPORTS

The techniques needed for camping and bushwalking represent basic skills that can be used when participating in other activities in the bush. 'Bush sports' combine a love of the natural environment with physical challenge. Because of environmental and/or safety concerns, not all activities are permitted or condoned in every national park or wilderness area, so always check with the relevant authorities when you are planning your trip. The most popular bush sports are abseiling, rock climbing, mountain biking, canoeing and caving.

Abseiling

Abseiling or rappelling is a skill developed by mountaineers to descend cliffs safely using a rope. The techniques used in abseiling form a key ability that can be transferred for use in many other bush sports, such as rock climbing, canyoning and caving. Abseiling is one of the most spectacular and adrenaline-charged ways to see some of Australia's wilderness.

The best way to learn abseiling is to sign up for a day course offered by a professional abseiling operator, such a High and Wild in Katoomba, New South Wales. Most professional operators supply their own equipment—including ropes, descenders, karabiners and harnesses—as well as a helmet for protection against falling rocks.

Abseiling locations
New South Wales
Blue Mountains National Park
Wollemi National Park
Morton National Park
Lord Howe Island / Balls Pyramid
Warrumbungles National Park

Northern Territory
Kakadu /Arnhem Land Escarpment

Queensland
Carnarvon National Park
Glasshouse Mountains
Mount Lindesay/Mount Barney

South Australia
Flinders Ranges National Park
Flinders Chase National Park: Kangaroo Island
Nullarbor Plain

Tasmania
Dolerite Ranges: Mount Wellington, Du Cane, Cradle Mountain
Quartzite Ranges: Western and Eastern Arthurs
Tasman Peninsula sea cliffs
Frenchmans Cap

Victoria
    Mount Arapiles
    Grampians: Gariwerd National Park
    Mount Buffalo
    Port Campbell: Shipwreck sea cliffs

Western Australia
    Stirling Range National Park–Bluff Knoll region

Rock climbing

Australia may have a reputation for being among the flattest continents on the planet but we also have some of the best rocks, crags, hills and mountains to challenge the climbing enthusiast. Whichever state you choose to go to there are literally hundreds of recognised climbing locations that attract local and international climbers. Most outdoor stores and bookshops sell guidebooks on Australian climbing locations that also provide information on climbing equipment and tips for beginners. The best way to get into climbing, however, is to join a course run by a professional, experienced climber and learn by doing. Local professionals can also be a great source of information about good climbs in the region, ranging from beginner through to advanced. In a course you can assess your climbing ability and set realistic goals. Rock climbing is a safe sport, and one that is undergoing a renaissance of interest.

The broad scope of climbing can be broken down into specific styles and approaches. Top roping is when the rope is fed through an anchor at the top of the climb, and a belayer may be placed at the bottom to take the slack off the rope as the climber ascends; bouldering is a form of climbing conducted close to the ground obviating a need for ropes; soloing is climbing without ropes; sport climbing, which in providing easy access and close-set bolts, pushes the need for speed to the limit—as opposed to the slower pace and thought involved in traditional rock climbing. Then there's indoor climbing in gyms that provide an artificial training ground to practice hand-holds and manoeuvres; and mountaineering, with its focus on longer, higher expeditions into snow, ice and glacier, and requiring its own specialist equipment and techniques. Other forms of the sport include lead climbing and aid climbing.

Climbing and the environment

Rockclimbing has been a popular activity in Australia since the 1950s, although the sport existed for a couple of decades before that. As such, there is now an established climbing culture with many books on the subject providing information on where the best climbs are and how to ascend them—at grades that can vary from 4 for easier scrambles, to 32 and higher for the full-on thrill-seekers. Grades can differ according to the technical complexity of climbing manoeuvres required, the strength and stamina needed, and just how risky or plain scary the ascent is.

The popularity of climbing as an outdoor sport has raised questions about its sustainability in relation to the natural environment. Today climbers pursue the sport in greater and greater numbers, in concentrated areas, and use any number of bolts and secures which, over time, will erode fragile cliffs and crag structures. Also, chalk marks from climbs can be aesthetically unpleasant to view. Rock climbing is an attempt to challenge and overcome nature, but this doesn't mean that care should not be taken in protecting the environment, not only for the benefit of the local flora and fauna but also for the pleasure of other rock climbers. Thus it is important that climbers adhere to an informal code of conduct: minimising disturbance to rocks, cliffs and vegetation; reducing, where safely possible, the use of bolts; and generally respecting the rights of other visitors to the national parks. This point is also applicable to the other bush sports of abseiling, canyoning and caving.

Climbing preparation

Rock climbing is a specialist sport that requires a high degree of strength and stamina. If it is to be enjoyed to the full, physical fitness is the key. General fitness training, which may include training with weights, stretching and cardiovascular exercises, will improve your endurance, flexibility, agility and strength. Climbing is a pull–push activity: the arms and back pull up and the legs push, with gravity itself as the countervailing force. Exercises to strengthen the arms, upper back and legs are essential to success. These should be combined with stretches to improve the flexibility of the muscles to accomplish various climbing manoeuvres and to prevent injury, plus cardiovascular exercises to improve the body's capacity for carrying oxygen. Forearm strength is important, and can be improved by squeezing squash balls or putty.

Climbing equipment

Rock climbing is impossible, and dangerous, without the correct specialist equipment. In addition to basic abseiling gear, such as karabiners, descenders and harnesses, a basic personal rock climbing kit may include friction boots, gloves, ropes, nuts and cams, bolt brackets and chalk bag. A kit like this is expensive to set up. Appropriate clothing should also be worn, protecting against the sun and the rough scraping of rock. While climbers can be as exhibitionistic as they want in the fashion stakes, beginners may not want to draw too much attention to their skills. Due consideration must be taken for the expected weather conditions. Fundamentally, the gear should preferably be new, of the highest quality, and lightweight. A good range of light, strong, specialist rock climbing equipment is now available.

Friction boots are light, tight fitting and made of high-friction rubber which grips the rock surface cleanly. They come in a diverse range, from slippers to solid boots, depending on the style of climb being attempted. All-rounder boots are recommended for first-timers. Ropes are made of nylon, which can stretch well and handle sudden fall shocks. They come in various widths, depending on whether they are used singly or with other ropes, and are generally 50 metres long. Nylon can deteriorate with exposure to sunlight and chemicals, and so should be stored in a dry, dark area. Care should also be taken to minimise general wear and tear on the ropes during use, and to inspect themregularly for nicks and holes that expose the inner core. The climbing rope should be attached directly to the harness, which envelopes the waist and legs. Nuts are wedge-shaped or rough hexagonally contoured metal rings that are designed to jam inside narrow cracks and holes in the rock, through which a rope can be fed or anchored. Cams are a modern version of nuts that are spring loaded to expand and grip inside various-sized hollows and fissures. The use and placement of nuts and cams in climbing is an art form in itself, with experienced climbers leaving no evidence of their climb.

Mountain biking

Mountain biking has emerged in Australia as one of the most popular recreational activities in national parks, state forests, and other public reserves. The growth of interest in this activity is related to two factors:

first, the appeal of discovering the national parks and their networks of logging roads, fire trails and four-wheel-drive tracks; and second, the technical evolution of the mountain bike that allows easy passage through the bush. Suspension forks, aluminium frames, quick-shifting indexed gears, and powerful cantilever brakes make mountain biking a reliable, safe, fun and easy activity. Aluminium, titanium, magnesium and carbon fibre are replacing steel and chrome-moly traditionally used for constructing the frame and forks. These materials are lighter and stronger, and have the potential to be cheaper.

The mountain bike possesses many advantages over walking. Much more can be seen in the same time because you travel at higher speeds, which makes mountain biking the perfect compromise between enjoying the scenery and arriving at your destination. More luggage can be carried in panniers than in a backpack, which allows longer trips to be planned.

The popularity of mountain biking as a wilderness activity raises important questions of environmental sustainability and sensibility. Biking should not be conducted in ecologically-sensitive wilderness locations, and bikers should be thoughtful towards the needs and activities of other visitors to the bush.

Equipment

Mountain bikes are by far the most popular type of bike sold, primarily because of their versatility. Cycling magazines are full of articles, reviews and advertisements for mountain bikes, and the international competitive mountain bike racing scene has quickly culminated in an officially recognised Olympic event.

Particular characteristics distinguish mountain bikes from touring bikes, racers, commuting hybrids, BMXs and stunt bikes:

- thick knobbly tires, usually of 26 inch diameter
- 24 or 27 indexed gears either by grip-shirt or rapid-fire levers
- adjustable suspension either on the front or on both wheels
- quick release wheels, brakes and seat posts for ease of use
- straight handlebars aligned perpendicular to the frame
- thick over-sized frame tubing made from light metal alloys.

In general, prices rise in inverse proportion to weight: choose a bike that balances lightweight comfort against how much you want to spend.

24 Some mountains can only be ascended with the aid of a rope.

25 Mt Banks, NSW, the ultimate big-wall rock climbing adventure: a sheer 510m.

26 Australia has over 35 000km of coastline to camp along.

27 Some camping trips can be
undertaken without tents—
huts are prevalent throughout
Australia's alpine regions.

28 Many caves can be explored
without the aid of a guide.

29 Despite their imposing size, most
web-weaving spiders are harmless.

32

30 Photographers can slow the flow
    of water in an image by using a
    long shutter speed.

31 Wards Canyon in Carnarvon
    National Park, QLD can be accessed
    without the aid of ropes.

32 Photographing the unique
    temperate flora of Tasmania.

33 The idyllic Beauchamp Falls, The Otways, Vic.

34 Hollands Gorge in The Budawang NSW.

35 Capertee Valley, Wollemi Nationa Park, NSW.

38

6 Barn Bluff in the Cradle Mountain–Lake St
  Clair National Park World Heritage
  Area, Tas.

7 Idyllic camping at Lawson,
  Blue Mountains, NSW.

8 Camping ground in the Wadbilliga
  National Park, NSW.

39 Canoeing on the upper Deua
    River, NSW.

40 Mt Ginini, The Brindabellas, ACT.

41 Deep Pass, Wollemi National Park,
    NSW.

42 Enjoying a rest in the morning,
    The Budawangs, NSW.

43

45

46

43 Most managed camping grounds have tables, fireplaces and toilets as standard facilities.

44 A mountain bike allows campers to access remote areas. Upper Mersey Valley, Tas.

45 Sometimes a rock overhang can substitute for a tent, such as in the Stirling Ranges, WA.

46 When camping at lookouts, what is gained in views is often lost in the lack of nearby water.

47 Many camping grounds in Australia can only be accessed using a four-wheel-drive vehicle.

48 Distance walking allows campers to access the wildest terrain. Lower Capertee Valley, NSW.

Ensure it has an adequate frame size so that the pedals can be reached without stretching and so that there is at least a 50-millimetre clearance between the top tube and your body when straddling the frame; that has quality groupset componentry (for example, Shimano XT or XTR sets of brakes, gears, cranks, hubs, handlegrips, chains and pedals); and that has thorn-proof tubes for handling rough conditions.

Important accessories include a helmet, a bidon cage for water bottles, a mountain bike pump that fits the valves, a repair kit, spare tubes with the correct valves to fit the rims, plus racks and panniers for carrying food and equipment. These accessories can be purchased and haggled over as part of the complete bike deal.

All in all, the outlay will be expensive for a new bike that will be both reliable and comfortable if regular mountain biking is intended. Any less, and safety will be sacrificed. There's nothing worse than walking an unrideable bike out of the wilderness along an endless flat track. If you plan to do overnight rides or venture into rugged terrain, an aluminium bike with front suspension should be the minimum considered.

Mountain biking locations
Australian Capital Territory
Brindabella Ranges
Namadgi National Park

New South Wales
Blue Mountains National Park
Wollemi National Park
Morton National Park
Kosciuszko National Park
Barrington Tops
Northern Territory
MacDonnell Ranges–Alice Springs region

Queensland
Scenic Rim (south and west of Brisbane)

South Australia
Adelaide Hills / Mount Lofty Ranges
Flinders Ranges National Park

Tasmania
Maria Island
South West National Park
Tasman Peninsula

Victoria
Alpine National Park
East Gippsland
Wilsons Promontory

Western Australia
South-western corner–Albany region (karri and jarrah forests)

Canoeing

The term canoeing includes a wide variety of water-based wilderness adventuring, such as flat water canoeing, whitewater kayaking and sea kayaking. Flat water canoeing is by far the most popular activity. It can be learned in a short time and opens up large areas of pristine wilderness that might otherwise be inaccessible. Whitewater kayaking is limited to rapids in the more mountainous regions in the eastern states and Tasmania and takes longer to master than flat water canoeing. Sea kayaking takes flat water canoeing out to sea where camps can be set up on isolated beaches.

Other water-based activities besides canoeing include li-loing and whitewater rafting. Li-loing is very popular in the gorges and canyons in the Blue Mountains in New South Wales, as well as canyons in Victoria, and can be pursued in a leisurely fashion on its own or as part of a more active abseiling/canyoning experience. Whitewater rafting trips are popular in many states. Some of the best locations are found in the Snowy Mountains, Tasmania and northern Queensland.

Equipment

The canoe is an open-decked craft that is paddled by a single blade oar. Kayaks were first developed by the Inuits—'kayak' is in fact an Inuit word— for travelling in bumpy seas and, as such, they are closed-deck crafts that are more aptly described as being worn rather than sat in. Kayaks use paddles with blades at both ends. While fibreglass is the most common material for the hulls of canoes and kayaks, some are made of a tough plastic to withstand bumps and impacts on rocks. Whitewater kayaks are much shorter than sea kayaks because they require much more manoeuvrability. The longer design of the sea kayak provides greater straight-line speed and the ability to carry heavier pack loads.

As always with outdoor activities, having the right equipment is essential for safety reasons, and for maximising enjoyment. Apart from the craft itself, canoeing may require the following:

- helmet
- personal flotation device (PDF) or buoyancy vest
- wetsuit and thermals for cold conditions
- sunscreen and sunglasses
- waterproof bags for keeping spare clothing and equipment dry.

A sturdy helmet can prevent head injuries from rocks and the canoe itself if capsized, and also against the stray paddling action of fellow canoeists. A cap worn under the helmet and the application of sunscreen will protect against the glare of the sun and from the reflections off the water. Wetsuits protect against the cold in deep canyon gorges and high mountain streams, but should be sleeveless to allow free arm movement. Gloves can prevent blisters forming on soft skin, and light footwear will protect the feet if the craft capsizes, leaving you with a soggy walk across the riverbed back to shore. Because of the tendency to get extremely wet in the pursuit of fun and adventure, a change of clothes should not be for- gotten. Sea kayaking opens up the possibility of using some fancy gadgets ranging from unisex skirts and water packs to sail rigs and emergency satellite distress beacons.

Basic techniques and tips

While flat water canoeing is relatively straightforward, the particular skills of whitewater kayaking and sea kayaking should be taught by a qualified instructor. Here are some basic tips for the beginner:

- To get into a canoe or kayak, lie the paddle flat across the craft as a brace between it and the shore.
- Keep the paddle as upright and vertical as possible during the stroke.
- Use your back and stomach muscles, as well as your arms, to push through the stroke. This will prevent early exhaustion in the arms.

- The craft steers not from the front but from the middle where you are. Turning a kayak can be achieved by a sweep stroke, which pushes the paddle through the water away from the hull.
- Most capsizes can be avoided by doing what doesn't come intuitively—that is, to continue paddling down the rapids instead of stopping. This provides additional stability. A slap stroke—hitting the water with the flat of the paddle blade on the fall side—can also prevent many capsizes.
- Practise capsize situations with a friend or instructor before handling the real thing. Getting used to these situations plus getting wet is a good way of releasing tension and overcoming unnecessary fears.
- Don't leave the canoe if you have capsized. It will inevitably float better than you will, and is more easily seen.
- Ensure your possessions are firmly attached to the canoe before paddling out.

Canoeing and kayaking locations
New South Wales
Blue Mountains National Park: Coxs River
Wollemi National Park: Colo River
Morton National Park: Shoalhaven River/Lake Yarrunga
Nepean/Hawkesbury River system
Kosciuszko National Park: Murray River, Thredbo, Snowy River
Barrington Tops: Williams River, Manning River, Hunter River
Nymboida National Park: Nymboida River
Guy Fawkes River National Park: Guy Fawkes River

Queensland
Tully River
Barron River
Mulgrave River
Cairns region: sea kayaking

Tasmania
Central Highlands
Forth/Mersey River systems
Franklin River
Gordon River
South West National Park
Huon River
Tasman Peninsula: sea kayaking

Victoria
    Alpine National Park
    East Gippsland
    Glenelg River

Western Australia
    Avon River

Caving

The bush typically invokes images of eucalyptus trees, lakes, rivers, pristine beaches and mountain ranges. Yet a fascinating world lies underneath all this surface glamour—the subterranean environment of caves, tunnels, shafts and underground rivers. For those who like to explore new frontiers, caving is ideal. Many cave systems in Australia have not yet been fully inspected, and many cave sites are no doubt still waiting to be discovered. The sport is, however, not for those who have qualms about closed-in spaces, squeezing underneath or between large rocks, getting wet and incredibly muddy, or—in the case of more advanced caving expeditions—scuba diving underground.

For very basic caving, all the equipment you need is a torch, overalls, a helmet and good boots. Many of the skills involved are similar to that of abseiling, with ropes, harness, karabiners and descender also required. There are additional dangers, such as sudden increases in the water level due to rain outside, toxic gases and total darkness.

For beginners there are some magnificent show-caves. The best-known are the Jenolan Caves in the western Blue Mountains, where many cave tours are guided. In remote national parks there are many self-guided caves. To enter the majority of caves, however, you need to obtain a permit from the local national parks authorities.

Caves are incredibly delicate environments, the dripping limestone-enriched water taking millions of years to build structures such as stalactites, stalagmites, shawls, helictites and curtains. These formations are very fragile, and so require that you take extra care.

Glossary of caving terms

Blind valley: A valley in which a stream sinks underground.

Cave coral: Speleothem formed by a splashing, or diffuse capillary flow.

Cave sediments: Material washed into the cave.

Doline: A closed depression produced by solution, subsidence and/or collapse.

Flowstone: Speleothem produced by degassing of thin films of water flowing over cave walls.

Helictite: Horizontal stalactite formed in stable cave environment where the rates of water percolation are so slow as to prevent drops forming.

Karst: A terrain of landforms remaining after bedrock erosion by natural waters.

Solution form: Small features such as pits and ripples in rock surface produced by water dissolving limestone.

Speleothem: Cave decoration such as stalactites etc.

Tufa: A porous deposit often containing organic material.

Prospective cavers are strongly advised to join a speleological society, club or association. Many of these organisations have their own web pages, while others have contact details linked to popular bushwalking sites. Some of the larger clubs are:

Blue Mountains Speleological Club
Southern Tasmanian Caverneers
Speleological Research Group of Western Australia Inc
Sydney University Speleological Society
Top End Speleological Society
University of Technology Sydney Speleological Society

Caving locations
New South Wales

Blue Mountains region: Jenolan, Church Creek, Wombeyan, Tuglow
Bungonia State Recreation Area (near Goulburn)
Kosciuszko National Park: Yarrangobilly, Cooleman Caves, Wee Jasper
Deua National Park: Marble Arch, Bendethera, Wyanbene
Wellington

South Australia
  Kelly Caves, Kangaroo Island
  Nullarbor Plain

Tasmania
  Hasting Caves
  Maracoopa Caves
  Exit Caves
  Vanishing Falls
  Mount Anne

Victoria
  Buchan

Western Australia
  Margaret River

LEISURE ACTIVITIES

Not all camping trips need be sports adventure holidays, and nor should they be. And even the most adventurous and energetic outdoor enthusiasts must have a backup plan when the weather turns nasty. Included here are a few leisurely pursuits particularly suited to camping in the bush, wherever you are.

Nature study

The Australian wilderness is unique in its extraordinary diversity of native flora and fauna; its landscapes and wildlife continuing the eternal process of adaptation and change as the island continent drifts further from the site of ancient Gondwana. Looking about us as we tramp and camp is like taking a snapshot of life, making stills from a movie that has been playing for over 150 million years. Prehistoric creatures roam freely in this land today—crocodiles, lizards, dragons and geckos—while trees of ages past, such as the Wollemi Pine which dates back to the days of the dinosaurs, are being rediscovered and propagated. With so much of the continent yet to be properly explored, from the ocean depths to isolated and impenetrable canyons and ravines, from the dry heart of the central deserts to the lush tropical rainforest canopies, who knows what natural secrets the land will eventually yield?

A better understanding of nature not only satisfies our intrinsic intellectual curiosity, but can also improve our practical outdoor and bushcraft skills. There are many books and college courses that can assist a novice naturalist, whether it be in studying geology, native flora or fauna, astronomy or predicting the weather. Even better is to join a club or society with similar interests that organises regular trips into the bush. There is so much to be learnt, to see and to discover.

Geology

Geology is the study of rocks which comprise the crust of the earth, the changes they have undergone, as well as the minerals from which they are made. Within this broad umbrella lie the specialised fields of petrology, mineralogy, geomorphology and palaeontology, to name a few. The Australian landscape provides excellent opportunities to explore an interest in geology and its related fields. You can observe many interesting types of rock and rock formations within short distances, whether it be long-since-cooled magma dykes of ancient volcanoes such as the Breadknife in the Warrumbungles, the spectacular sedimentary sandstone cliffs and gorges that run the length of the Blue Mountains, the magnificent limestone caves caused by running water eroding softer rock, or the imposing dolerite rock formations along the Tasmanian coast. Inspection of rock formations can reveal not only the history of movements and erosion in the earth's crust, but can also—through the accumulations of peat, coal, organically formed limestone deposits and even fossils—reveal the rich history of plants and animals that have lived on this continent over the millennia.

Flora

Several books have now been published to assist plant identification based on readily observable characteristics such as the shape of the flower, the fruit or leaves. From the basic skills of identification come the broader issues of understanding ecosystems, how plants interact with animals and the environment to sustain life, as well as identifying the landscape types such as closed and open woodlands, forests, shrub lands, alpine regions, wetlands, marshes and deserts. From this knowledge comes more practical skills: the ability to find the easiest passage through rough terrain, to locate water and bush foods in an emergency, and to identify particular animals, plants and landforms of interest and significance.

Fauna

In a quiet campsite, under the cover of darkness, the marsupials: possums and bandicoots fidget in the trees and search the grounds for snacks and treats, the more cheeky ones going so far as to undo straps and zips on rucksacks in the course of their foraging. The adaptability of many bird species has allowed them to colonise every type of habitat on the Australian continent, from the sand and spinifex of the desert to the deepest tropical rainforests. The best times for viewing birds is early in the morning and late in the afternoon, when they congregate and feed. Reptiles are most active when the weather is warmest, using the midday sun to heat their cold-blooded bodies.

Researching and studying Australian animals and their behaviour can help you locate and observe them when you are in the bush and, again, there are many books that can provide such information (see Appendix VIII, page 127). Knowledge of animal tracks and trace signs will help you identify the local wildlife when it cannot be seen. Binoculars are handy in studying Australian fauna—there are few wild creatures that will voluntarily approach people, but by being quiet, still and attentive, many creatures will go about their day oblivious to the attention. Walking softly and steadily along bush tracks will inevitably reward you with surprise meetings, from snakes and lizards to the rarer species of birds and mammals.

Photography

Camping and bushwalking can take you into the most spectacular locations, and capturing the scenery on film can be a rewarding exercise, both artistically and financially. High-quality photographs can be taken from any camera, and with advances in lens technology there is less quality loss through using adjustable zoom lenses as opposed to bringing along several fixed focal length lenses. As with most art, the quality of the work increases with practice and experimentation. A heavy and expensive camera is no shortcut to success; it is the eye and the skill of the photographer which produce truly great work. Robert Rankin's *Wilderness Light* is an excellent non-technical book that discusses composition, subject and lighting aspects of photography in national parks.

Camera

A basic 35 mm SLR camera that has manual settings to compensate for measuring inaccuracies in the light meter or for achieving particular photographic effects is recommended. Fog, high contrast, direct sunlight, the position of subject and long shadows can all lead to incorrect exposure evaluations. A manual mode provides the photographer with more control over pictures of waterfalls and other time exposure shots. Amateur wilderness photographers with commercial aspirations may consider upgrading to medium format (for example, a 6 cm x 7 cm) image to provide maximum magazine-quality definition.

Tripod

A tripod should be considered a mandatory accessory when taking a camera into the bush. Dimly-lit rainforest canopies, narrow valleys, flowing river shots, and waterfalls all require time exposures of anything up to 30 seconds. 'Camera-shake' can occur at shutter speeds below one-sixtieth of a second, blurring an otherwise beautiful shot. Professional landscape photographers don't take any risks, even on reasonably high shutter speeds. If there is no space for a tripod, a forked tree or well-positioned boulder, even a rucksack or bundle of clothes can prove a handy substitute.

Lenses

Ideally a standard fixed lens (50 mm), a macro (24 mm), and a telephoto (100 mm or 200 mm) will give optimal results because the number of glass elements in the lens is kept to a minimum, thereby allowing maximum resolution. Generally, the lower the minimum f-stop—for example, f 1.8—of the lens, the greater its quality. But there is also the convenience/weight trade-off to consider with carting along several expensive lenses through the rugged outdoor environment. Despite having a higher f-stop, a good zoom lens will do the job of many lenses and still give more than adequate definition. Many SLR camera bodies come with a 28–80 mm lens as a standard option, and this provides more than enough variation in focal length for a diverse range of outdoor photographs. A little walking and repositioning can sometimes prove a worthwhile substitute for an expensive 300 mm telephoto lens.

Filters

Adding a filter to the lens can provide some interesting effects, or correct hazy light or reflection. Polarising filters can add colour and depth to lakes and coasts by blocking reflection of the sun's rays, as well as accentuating the deep blue of an outback sky. However, they reduce the amount of light entering the camera by up to two f-stops and they become less useful when there is diffused light. Windy, fresh conditions ensure a minimum of haze over landscapes so most of the time a skylight or UV filter is unnecessary. Some forest vistas, however, can get extremely hazy on hot calm days. In such conditions, a polarising filter will help to make features more defined.

Film

Although the quality gap between negative and slide film is narrowing, transparency—reversal, slide or positive—films still produce the best results in terms of colour saturation and resolution. Aim to use low ASA-rated films, because they have minimal grain and can most faithfully reproduce nature's colours. Lower ASA films are slower, however, requiring longer exposure times, which may necessitate the use of a tripod even in conditions of bright sunshine.

Slide films have their disadvantages, however. They are usually more expensive, the results are more difficult to view, and there is limited scope for corrections during processing. Exposures have to be spot-on for slide film, whereas with negative film you can make alterations up to two f-stops. The superb quality afforded by slide film, however, makes it hard to beat for magazine-quality reproduction. At the end of the day, choose the film that suits the purpose or take a range of film.

Astronomy

In the city environment, the night skies are obscured by increasing light and air pollution. It is only in wilderness areas that the true majesty of the stars and constellations which rule the night skies above can be properly appreciated. For this reason many campers and bushwalkers often pack a pair of binoculars or even a small telescope and mounting for celestial observation. The views are simply stupendous: the southern skies above Australia provide a bounty of stars, planets, nebulae, globular clusters, comets, meteorites and artificial satellites for the amateur astronomer to gaze upon. The immense vastness of the Milky Way and beyond into interstellar space is an awe-inspiring sight, reminding us of just how small a part of the universe we are.

You do not need expensive equipment to enjoy the science of astronomy. The bright haze of the Milky Way and many of the stars, planets and constellations are observable with the naked eye. Proper identification can be made with the help of star charts and maps, which are readily available from most astronomical societies, interest groups, astronomy magazines and bookstores. (See Appendix VIII, page 127.)

Binoculars and telescopes

A good pair of binoculars for general astronomical purposes should ideally be small and light, and with a magnification of between 6 and 10 times. Binoculars are easier to carry than telescopes, do not require mounts or tripods, and can be used to observe other features of the bush, such as animals or terrain. The disadvantage with binoculars, however, is that they have a far lower magnification than telescopes.

Telescopes come in two basic types—refractors and reflectors—although expensive combination designs called catadioptric telescopes are also available. Refractors are the earliest type and date back to the seventeenth century, and were used by pioneers such as Galileo. They work by allowing rays of light to pass from the object through a specially shaped lens called an object-glass. These rays of light are focused, then the image is magnified by a second lens known as the eyepiece or ocular. The function of the object-glass is to collect light and, generally, the bigger the lens, the more powerful the refractor telescope.

Reflectors work on a slightly different principle. Light passes down an open tube where it is reflected by a parabolically curved mirror at the far end onto another mirror placed at 45 degrees. The light from this second mirror is then directed into the eyepiece. Both types of telescope have their advantages and disadvantages. Refractors produce false colour because when visible light is bent through the object-glass, the longer wavelengths are bent less sharply than the shorter wavelengths, and so these differing waves are brought into focus in a different place. This effect can be removed by adding more lenses, at the expense of reducing the amount of light reaching the eyepiece.

That said, the refractors are, aperture for aperture, considered more effective than reflectors, although generally more expensive. For reasons such as cost and convenience, many amateur astronomers choose reflector telescopes —in particular, the Newtonian reflector—over refractors to take with them into the bush.

Mountings

Just as important as the telescope itself is the choice of mount on which to place it. Mounts come in various types for different purposes, and it is important for the bushwalker or camper to consider factors such as weight and encumbrance. Telescopic mounts serve to keep the telescope pointing at the desired object over time and for stability and clarity. The most common mounting system is equatorial mounting, where one axis points to the celestial pole, and is therefore parallel to the earth's axis of rotation. With a clockwork or motorised drive, the telescope can then track any celestial object by rotating along this axis.

This is also handy for photography—by attaching a camera without a lens to the telescope in place of the eyepiece, you essentially have an incredibly large telephoto by which to photograph eclipses, the surface of the moon, constellations, star clusters and nebulae. Any ordinary 35 mm film will capture these images, but long exposure times are called for and, without equatorial mounting, the resulting image will contain streaking effects as the stars continue in their path across the night sky.

Other pursuits

The only limit here is your own sense of imagination. From activities such as landscape drawing and painting to in-tent games of cards and chess on rainy afternoons; keeping a journal of your camping trips, or even working on that novel-in-progress; bush or beach cricket with no boundaries in sight; re-enacting legendary medieval battles; napping; poetry nights; ghost stories; impromptu pantomimes; campfire debates on life, the universe and everything; testing friendships by telling, at length, the story of your life, or repeating the worst jokes you've ever heard; or even searching for the legendary savage drop-bears.

Binocular and telescope performance and magnification

Binoculars are specified by designations such as 6 x 30 or 8 x 40. The first number is the magnification and the second is the size of the aperture in millimetres; that is, the size of the front lenses. When purchasing binoculars, remember that although higher magnification is good, the enlargement of an image also means that it will become dimmer because the captured light is spread over a greater area. The only way to maintain a bright image with higher magnification is to increase the size of the aperture, which may mean buying a bigger, heavier and more expensive pair. Larger apertures with the same magnification, conversely, make dim images much brighter. Choose a pair that balances your needs. Keep in mind also that magnifications of 10 or higher will generally require a mount to keep the image steady. If you want this kind of magnification for astronomical observation, you may want to start thinking about a small telescope.

The performance of a **telescope** hinges on two factors: its aperture and the focal length of the object-glass or main mirror. Aperture determines the faintest objects that can be viewed, while focal length determines the size of the image: its field of view. Image quality, however, can depend on many factors, including local atmospheric conditions, the optical quality of the telescope itself and the eyesight of the user. Focal ratios (f-ratios), instead of focal lengths, are often used to describe telescopic performance. This is the focal length divided by the aperture. Generally, telescopes with low f-ratios have a wider field of view; long f-ratios mean a larger image size, but a smaller field of view. Telescopes with f-ratios of f/6 to f/8 make good all-round instruments. Magnification is calculated by dividing the focal length of the telescope by the focal length of its eyepiece. Most telescopes have interchangeable eyepieces to allow for extended or close-up views. Again, while using an eyepiece with a short focal length will increase magnification, it will also dim the image by spreading the captured light over a wider area. As only larger apertures can compensate for this effect, it is a general rule of thumb only to use magnifications up to twice the size of the aperture.

8

Classic Camping: It doesn't get any better than this

Australia is blessed with an extraordinary variety of beautiful, idyllic camping localities. Ancient rainforests that border coral reefs, mist-enshrouded coastal ranges, jagged quartzite peaks, pristine lakes and rivers, dissected rocky canyons, towering eucalypt woodlands and lofty snowgum-covered plateaus are just some of the landscapes that make camping pleasant in its own right.

Campers will disagree wildly about what constitutes the ideal spot. Is it the proximity to water? The view? The shade? The grassy ground? Is there protection from the elements? Is it easy to access, yet still remote? Are there walking tracks to interesting areas? These are all important elements and are given different priorities by different people. The perfection of a camp site will also be influenced by the weather, the company, the popularity and other nearby highlights. What can be a cherished place for one person can be deemed hell by another.

What follows is a listing of a few classic camping areas for each state, sorted into what's accessible for vehicles and those areas restricted to walkers only. Since there are over 1700 official managed campsites in Australia, let alone the infinite variety of bushwalking sites, this listing is by no means comprehensive, nor are the areas rated by any objective or subjective criteria. On page 108, we've listed our own Top 10 camping areas—just for the record.

Australian Capital Territory

Residents of Canberra are fortunate that the nation's capital is encircled by high-quality parkland. In fact, almost two-thirds of the Australian Capital Territory is encompassed by Namadgi National Park, which borders the largest park in New South Wales—Kosciuszko. The terrain is fairly mountainous and parts of the Brindabella Range are snowbound in winter. Take warm clothing at all times of the year. Snow chains may be required in winter, and most alpine roads are subject to seasonal closure. The eastern foothills of the Brindabellas provide the catchment area of Canberra's water supply, so camping is prohibited there. A short drive east from Canberra takes you to the spectacular Budawangs and the Deua/Wadbilliga National Parks system back in New South Wales—renowned for their wild and remote terrain.

Few people realise that picturesque Jervis Bay and its national park are part of the Australian Capital Territory. A recent addition to Australia's marine parks, Jervis Park offers a number of popular camping areas with a high standard of facilities.

Vehicle access
Jervis Bay: several coastal sites including Cave Beach
Mount Ginini, Brindabella Range, Namadgi National Park
Mount Clear (Naas Creek), Namadgi National Park
Orroral Campground, Namadgi National Park

Walkers only
Mount Gingera, Brindabella Range
Pryors Hut, Brindabella Range

New South Wales

Despite the state's relatively high population density, New South Wales contains a large number of high-quality camping environments of an almost unbelievable diversity—from outback desert dunes to dense subtropical rainforest, from alpine glacial lakes to dissected sandstone plateaus, and from forests of giant eucalypts to gorgeous coastal coves. There's something to please everyone.

The climate is generally mild and camping is possible all year around. Take note that peak times are Easter and the Christmas holidays, and many campsites get overloaded. Also remember that fees apply on many officially managed areas that contain facilities. Rangers patrol these grounds to ensure campers comply with the regulations.

Vehicle access

Bendethera, Deua National Park (4WD)

Blue Waterholes (Cooleman Caves), northern Kosciuszko National Park

Boyd River Crossing, Danangra Boyd National Park

Dunn's Swamp (Kandos Weir), western Wollemi National Park

Euroka Clearing, lower Blue Mountains

Manning River Camping Area, Barrington Tops State Forest

Mulligans Hut, Gibraltar Range

Murphys Glen, Blue Mountains National Park

Newnes, south-western Wollemi National Park

The Big Hole, Barrington Tops (seasonal 4WD access only)

The Cascades Rest Area (Tuross River), Wadbilliga National Park (4WD)

Wattle Flat, Styx River State Forest, New England plateau

White Rock Camping Area, Chichester State Forest, Barrington Tops

Yadboro, Clyde River (southern Budawangs), Yadboro State Forest

Walkers only

Blue Gum Forest (Acacia Flat), Grose Gorge, Blue Mountains National Park

Burning Palms, Royal National Park

Capertee River (lower), Wollemi National Park

Clyde River (upper), southern Morton National Park

Gunnoomooroo Camp, southern Warrumbungles National Park

Kowmung River (middle), Kanangra-Boyd National Park

Ku-ring-gai Chase National Park (ferry access also)

Lake Yarrunga, northern Morton National Park (also canoe access)

Marley Beach, Royal National Park

McArthurs Flat, Nattai National Park

Newtons Beach (and coves beyond), Nadgee Nature Reserve, south-eastern NSW

Platypus Creek, New England National Park

Valentine Hut, Kosciuszko National Park (mountain bike access also)

Wollemi Creek (lower), eastern Wollemi National Park

Northern Territory

Camping in the Top End and the red centre is very much a seasonal affair—for one-half of the year it's hot and wet, the other it's dry and mild. Fortunately, tourists visiting the internationally renowned attractions in their millions rarely camp outdoors, leaving the territory's many camping areas relatively empty. Self-sufficiency is essential in such remote country. Four-wheel-drive vehicles, particularly travelling in convoys, are highly recommended as the best way to camp here, as is carrying ample quantities of water, because fresh sources can be few and far between.

Vehicle access

Boggy Hole, Finke River (4WD access)

Ellery Creek Big Hole, West Macdonnell National Park

Four Mile Hole, Kakadu National Park

Frontier Kings Canyon, Watarrka National Park

Kambolgie, Kakadu National Park

Leliyn (Edith Falls) Campground, Nitmiluk (Katherine Gorge) National Park

Nitmiluk Visitor Centre, Nitmiluk (Katherine Gorge) National Park

Palm Creek, Finke Gorge National Park (4WD access)

Serpentine Chalet Bush Camping Area, West Macdonnell National Park

Surprise Creek, Litchfield National Park

Trephina Creek (opposite Bluff), Trephina Gorge Nature Park

Woodland Camping Area, West Macdonnell National Park

Walkers only

Seventeen Mile Falls, Nitmiluk (Katherine Gorge) National Park

Biddlecombe Cascades, Nitmiluk (Katherine Gorge) National Park

Crystal Falls, Nitmiluk (Katherine Gorge) National Park

Edith River Crossing, Nitmiluk (Katherine Gorge) National Park

Eighth Gorge, Nitmiluk (Katherine Gorge) National Park

Sweetwater Pool, Nitmiluk (Katherine Gorge) National Park

Queensland

More national parks have been declared in Queensland than any other state, however, the range of camping areas isn't as diverse as New South

Wales and Victoria. Tropical rainforest dominates many of the coastal parks and the damp dark humid conditions are hardly conducive to ideal camping. The best car-based camping in Queensland is probably on Fraser Island because of the abundance of freshwater lakes so close to the beaches. The lovely Carnarvon National Park is literally an oasis in an otherwise dry interior.

Despite popular conceptions, the majority of the islands on the Great Barrier Reef don't have large-scale commercial resorts. Boat-based camping is becoming very popular. Like the Northern Territory, Cape York Peninsula is subject to intense seasonal fluctuations in rainfall and most of the dirt roads in this remote and rugged area become impassable during the summer wet season.

Vehicle access

Blue Lagoon, Moreton Island (4WD access)
Broadwater, Sundown National Park, southern Queensland
Coochin Creek, Beerburrum State Forest
East Claudie River, Iron Range National Park (4WD access)
Freshwater Camping Area, Cooloola National Park (4WD access)
Green Mountains Camping Area, Lamington National Park
McKenzie/Allom/Boomanjin lakes camping areas, Fraser Island (4WD access)
Mission Point, Bribie Island National Park (boat and 4WD access)
Mount French, Moogerah Peaks National Park
Noah Beach, Daintree National Park, Cape Tribulation (4WD recommended)
Purling Brook Falls, Springbrook National Park
Spicers Gap, Main Range National Park
Spotted Gum Camping Area, Expedition National Park

Walkers only

Big Bend, Carnarvon National Park, central Queensland
Cedar Bay, Cedar Bay National Park
Goochee Lagoon, Great Sandy National Park, northern Fraser Island
Mount Barney saddle (closed seasonally), south-eastern Queensland
Mount Bartle Frere, Bellenden Ker National Park, northern Queensland
Mulligans Bay, Hinchinbrook Island
Noosa River (lower), southern Cooloola National Park
Zoe Bay, Hinchinbrook Island

South Australia

Without the Flinders Ranges, camping opportunities would be pretty sparse in South Australia. In addition to the fascinating geological section of the national park centred on Wilpena Pound, there are also the Gammon Ranges to the north and Mount Remarkable to the south. Unfortunately, camping opportunities in the Adelaide Hills are fairly ordinary. The other quality destination in the state is Kangaroo Island, rich in wildlife and pleasant coastal scenery.

The state is extremely dry, so plenty of water needs to be carried by campers. April to September is the best time to visit the interior. Many inland parks are accessible only by four-wheel-drive vehicle.

Vehicle access

Arcoona Creek and Bluff, western Gammon Ranges (4WD recommended)
Arkaroola, Arkaroola–Mount Painter Sanctuary
Aroona Valley Camp, Flinders Ranges National Park
Blue Gum Flat, Mount Remarkable National Park
Brachina Gorge, Flinders Ranges National Park
Bunyeroo Gorge, Flinders Ranges National Park
Cactus Beach, Nullarbor Plain
Coorong National Park
Dalhousie Springs, Witjira National Park
Howash Bend, Murray River (Morgan District)
Ippinitchie Campground, Wirrabara Forest
Memory Cove Wilderness Area, Lincoln National Park, Jussieu Peninsula
Rocky River, Flinders Chase National Park
Stokes Bay, northern Kangaroo Island
Western River Cove, northern Kangaroo Island

Walkers only

Cooinda Camp, Wilpena Pound, Flinders Ranges National Park
Grindells Hut, Gammon Ranges National Park
Kingfisher Flat, Mount Remarkable National Park
Mount McKinlay Springs, Gammon Ranges National Park
Ravine des Casoars, Flinders Chase National Park, Kangaroo Island
Wilkawillina Gorge, eastern Flinders Ranges National Park

Tasmania

Compact, mountainous, and wild, it is little wonder that Tasmania is the birthplace of the modern Australian conservation movement. Even though the state comprises less than one per cent of the area of the country, Tasmania contains probably the best-quality recreational wilderness areas.

The rugged topography, the pristine rivers, and some of the tallest forests in the world are preserved in World Heritage areas. The walking is generally hard-grade and self-sufficiency is paramount.

Campers should be prepared for appalling weather, and this would be the state's worst feature—it can literally rain for months. February is the best time to visit, when the weather in the spectacular south-west wilderness is most stable.

Vehicle access

Blue Stone Bay, Freycinet Peninsula, east coast
Cockle Creek, far south Tasmania
Fortescue Bay, Tasman Peninsula
Franklin River, Lyell Highway
Labillardiere camping area, southern Bruny Island
Lake Gordon (4WD recommended)
Lake Rowallan (southern section), Mersey River district
Lime Bay, Tasman Peninsula
Rocky Cape, Rocky Cape National Park, north coast
Springlawn Beach, Asbestos Range National Park
Styx River, Maydena district, central Tasmania
Waterhouse Point, north-east coast

Walkers only

Bryans Beach, Freycinet National Park
Cooks Beach, Freycinet National Park
Cracroft Crossing, South-West National Park
Darlington, Maria Island (ferry access)
Encampment Cove, Maria Island isthmus (ferry access)
Fotheringate Bay, Strzelecki National Park, Flinders Island
Hanging Lake, Eastern Arthurs, South-West National Park
Heritage Falls campsite, Douglas-Apsley National Park
Lake Cygnus, Western Arthur Range, South-West National Park

Lake Vera, Franklin–Gordon Wild Rivers National Park
Pine Valley, southern Cradle Mountain–Lake Saint Clair National Park
Pool of Bethesda, Walls of Jerusalem National Park
Scott-Kilvert Hut, Cradle Mountain–Lake Saint Clair National Park
South-East Cape, South-West National Park

Victoria

The Alpine National Park, despite its history of grazing, logging and ski development, is still one of the great natural reserves in the country. Extensive in size, the park offers an almost infinite number of quality wild bush-camping locations, as well as hundreds of officially managed sites. Much of the area is snowbound in winter.

The Grampians are the prime destination in the west. Together with the Otways and various smaller parks near Melbourne, these areas are managed carefully and consequently there are strict regulations on fees, fires and permits.

By contrast, the wilderness coast between Mallacoota and Sale in the east of the state, as well as the Lower Glenelg region between Portland and Nelson in the far west, are relatively untouched. To escape the crowds, the desert parks of Wyperfield and Hattah Lakes offer outback-style camping without having to drive for days.

Victorians are great lovers of the outdoors and because the state is small and densely populated, camping localities such as the Howqua River and Wilsons Promontory can easily become overcrowded. Choose your time of year very carefully.

Vehicle access

Aire River, Otways
Buandik, south-western Grampians (Geriwerd National Park)
Errinundra River, eastern Errinundra Plateau
Howqua River, Bindaree Hut and upstream, Mansfield district
Jerusalem Inlet campsites (numerous), Lake Eildon State Park
Keppel Hut, Marysville State Forest
Lake Albacutya, Wyperfield region, western Victoria
Lake Catani, Buffalo National Park
Lake Cobbler, Alpine National Park (4WD access)

Lake Mournpall, Hattah Lakes National Park
Lakeside Camping Area, Fraser National Park
Point Hicks, Croajingolong National Park
Shipwreck Creek, Croajingolong National Park, East Gippsland
Wingen Inlet, Croajingolong National Park

Walkers only

Feathertop (Bungalow Spur), Alpine National Park
First Wannon Creek, Major Mitchell Plateau, Grampians (Geriwerd National
  Park)
Jawbone Peak, Cathedral Range State Park
Lake Tali Karng, Alpine National Park
MacAlister Springs, Alpine National Park
Murray River (headwaters), Cobberas–Tingaringy region, East Gippsland
Post and Rail Camp, Lower Glenelg National Park, Nelson–Portland district
Seal Cove, Croajingolong National Park, East Gippsland
Sealers Cove, Wilsons Promontory National Park
Wonnangatta Valley, eastern Victoria

Western Australia

Comprising one-third of the country, Western Australia is open, dry and flat land. The northern half is subject to seasonal tropical weather patterns, and would constitute Australia's most remote region. Well-equipped, serious four-wheel drives with long-range fuel tanks and hundreds of litres of water are needed to explore the vast Kimberley and Pilbara regions.

The most accessible and pleasant area of this massive state is the southwest corner, which is dominated by tall stands of jarrah and karri forests. The coastal parks around Albany, especially the Nuyts Wilderness offer outstanding camping opportunities for adventurers along the recently realigned Bibbulmun Track.

Vehicle access

Chester Pass, Stirling Range National Park
Crossing Pool, Millstream-Chichester National Park
Deep Reach Pool, Millstream-Chichester National Park

Lucky Bay, Cape Le Grand National Park
Moingup Springs, Stirling Range National Park
Peaceful Bay, Walpole district, south coast
Snake Creek, Millstream-Chichester National Park
Weano Camping Area, Karijini (Hamersley Range) National Park

Walkers only

Bibbulmun Track
Fitzgerald River coastal coves, Fitzgerald River National Park
Third Arrow, Stirling Range National Park

Our Top 10: The best campsites in Australia

1   Encampment Cove, Maria Island isthmus, Tasmania
2   Bendethera, upper Deua River, Deua National Park, New South Wales
3   Lake Tali Karng, Alpine National Park, Victoria
4   Big Bend, Carnarvon National Park, central Queensland
5   The Big Hole, Barrington Tops, New South Wales
6   Eighth Gorge, Nitmiluk (Katherine Gorge) National Park, Northern Territory
7   Mount Clear (Naas Creek), Namadgi National Park, Australian Capital
      Territory
8   Deep Reach Pool, Millstream-Chichester National Park, Western Australia
9   Lake Cobbler, Alpine National Park, Victoria
10 Western River Cove, north Kangaroo Island, South Australia

9

The Future of Camping

The camper of the future will be barely recognisable from the bushwalking and conservationist pioneers of the Depression years. Several aspects of camping especially have undergone enormous change. By extrapolating the trends, we can envision what equipment future campers will use and what practices they will follow. Many of the modern, environmentally-aware camping regulations had their origins in Tasmania. This is because of the World Heritage Area status of many of that state's national parks and their unique, sensitive vegetation and rugged topography. A number of camping practices have changed markedly in the last few years and are still evolving.

Campfires

Once regarded as an essential component of the camping experience, the campfire is fast becoming a luxury. The policy of banning campfires was initially quite controversial when it was first introduced in alpine areas, especially in south-west Tasmania. There was a lot of discussion in the bushwalking magazines and newsletters at the time, but these days it is accepted as common practice and in the interest of all. At the time of writing, the ban on campfires includes officially gazetted wilderness areas, some coastal areas, and especially sensitive or overused areas in national parks and nature reserves throughout the country, such as Lake Tali Karng in Victoria and the Stirling Ranges in Western Australia.

The reasoning behind these bans is the important motivation to prevent the effects of bushfires on environmentally sensitive areas. For example, in Tasmania since 1960, fires have destroyed 16 per cent of alpine flora and eight per cent of rainforest. Several of the species that belong to these communities, such as the Huon pine, the King Billy pine, the pencil pine and the deciduous beech, do not regenerate. One fire started at a campsite in December 1980 on the northern shore of Lake Vera and burnt out 6450 hectares of the Franklin-Lower Gordon Wild Rivers National Park. The hut located there, as with the many huts along the Overland Track, now has coal supplied for heating.

Peat soils are particularly vulnerable to fire. Peat covers extensive areas of western Tasmania and is the very early stages of coal beds. It is made up of decomposed, compressed organic matter, is dark, greasy, and feels springy if walked on. Fires can burn down into the soil and smoulder for months, serving as potential ignition sources during future hot, dry weather. There are fines for lighting a fire on peat soil, whether it is inside or outside a designated fuel stove area.

Banning campfires and imposing a hefty penalty reduces the likelihood of native trees being cut down for wood. Doing so expands small clearings into larger ones, leaving visual scarring. People will no longer use fires as a rubbish place. Since impractically large, intense fires are needed to disintegrate rubbish, park rangers have found campsites are left with any amount of half-burnt rubbish. The residues from campfires also leave a scarring on the landscape that can take years to erase.

Thus, the campsite of the future will most probably not contain a fire. But it will be a cleaner, more pristine place.

Technology

High technology is already reaching the camping world, much to the disgust of the puritans. Part of the intrinsic motivation of venturing into the wilderness is to escape civilisation, but there remains the need to ensure that the trip is as safe and comfortable as possible.

The following equipment may eventually become regarded as compulsory, just as inflatable mattresses have become today.

Altimeters/Barometers—These electronic devices have been reduced in size to such an extent that they can now fit in a digital watch. They are useful for two purposes: as an aid to weather forecasting, and as a handy navigation device when cross-referencing your position on a map.

Global Positioning Systems (GPS)—The Rolls Royce of navigational devices, these are compasses, altimeters and map pin-pointers all rolled up in one. They can even calibrate the estimated time to your destination and your present, average and maximum ground speed. No doubt they can ensure you're not navigationally challenged when out in trackless terrain, but they do remove some of the risk element and therefore some of the adventure. The use of GPS begs the philosophical question as to whether it is desirable that everything is known and controlled.

Mobile/satellite phone—An even more contentious point is the use of communications equipment. Is wilderness integrity comprised when you can have a chat with friends or work colleagues back in civilisation? On the other hand, the mobile phone can no doubt save lives by calling in assistance in the event of a serious injury.

Laptop computers—The continued miniaturisation of computer technology will no doubt allow laptops, or perhaps palmtops, to be carried in a backpack. Imagine the possibilities: download maps and satellite images of the next day's route; access a vast library of botanical, zoological and geological information giving background information on everything you encounter; record diary entries; communicate with others; keep abreast of news and current affairs; store digital photographs; and obtain the latest weather forecasts. Your boss might even believe you're still at home working away on that report.

Space-age membranes—Fabrics will no doubt get stronger, lighter, more breathable and more waterproof. Single-wall tents needing no fly are already on the market, as well as Gore-Tex sleeping bag liners. In addition, self-supporting tents needing no pegs or guy ropes, and thereby minimising the damage to the ground, are endorsed by park authorities. Such tents can be pitched on rock platforms or soft sand, surfaces that are generally impractical for normal tents.

The law

The demand on our national parks has dramatically, throughout the latter half of the 20th century, increased due to a variety of factors:

- Population growth, albeit slowly
- Rapidly changing employment structures have led to increased leisure time
- There's a greater emphasis on fitness and health in today's society
- The publication of a plethora of guidebooks and magazines on outdoor recreational activities have armed visitors with intimate knowledge of the national parks.

Hence the need for comprehensive management policies to regulate our behaviour in national parks and nature reserves.

Fees– The widespread adoption of public spending rationalisation has led to a user-pays system so that fees are now being charged not only to enter popular national parks but also for camping and walking. The justification for applying fees is that they help pay for the upkeep of park facilities such as pit toilets, firewood and brochures, whether or not campers want or use these things.

Permits– In order to keep statistics on the number of people entering a particular national park, park authorities are increasingly using permits. For example, in Nadgee Nature Reserve in southern New South Wales, permits are required for all overnight activities. The granting of a permit is entirely at the discretion of the park authorities.

Quotas– Even more draconian than permits, quotas are the next step in the progression. If park authorities deem a particular area too environmentally sensitive for a mass onslaught of visitors, they'll restrict access to a set amount each year, or at any one time. This measure has already been adopted in some especially ecologically sensitive nature reserves, such as Memory Cove Wilderness Area in South Australia.

Fines–Today there are fines for fires, camping or walking without a permit, and for entering restricted areas. These can range from a ban on the future issuing of permits to the perpetrator in the case of minor infringements, to hefty $10,000 fines for major breaches. Criminal prosecution can even ensue if a fire is lit or attempted to be lit during total fire bans, particularly if it leads to property damage or loss of life.

Bans–The ultimate policy–totally forbidding entry into a national park or wilderness region–is being debated, and in some especially sensitive areas has already been considered. Some management practices almost adopt this philosophy today, by the closing and rehabilitation of access roads, or by banning overnight trips when they are the only practical means of seeing an area.

Other camping practices

Future campers, not knowing any different, will grow accustomed to policies that today we would consider draconian. It doesn't hurt to speculate about what other rules we might live under.

Sanitation—The accumulated effect of human faeces might lead to a systematic policy that everything is to be carried out. Difficult to enforce.

First aid—To encourage self-sufficiency and reduce rescue expenses, bushwalkers might have to do a first aid course before receiving a permit.

Navigation—Bushwalkers might have to pass a navigation exam before being allowed to venture into remote areas. A certain level of minimum physical fitness might also be evaluated. Don't laugh—scuba diving used to be unregulated, now fitness is a condition upon obtaining a Professional Association of Diving Instructors (PADI) certificate.

Party size—Minimum and maximum group sizes might be stipulated and enforced before walkers are allowed to venture out.

Checkpoints—To ensure that walkers are following their intended route, they might have to punch an identification card into key checkpoints along the route that transmits a signal back to park headquarters. This would allow rescuers to correctly identify which area to search in.

Tent selection—To reduce the damage caused by hammering in pegs and camping on soft wet soils, special tent designs will allow campers to pitch camp on terrain less likely to be disturbed by traffic. Free standing/self-supporting tents will probably become the norm.

Footwear—The use of soft rubber-soled shoes minimises impact damage to fragile plants and thus might one day be enforced by park authorities.

It is likely that campers of the future will look back on their forebears' methods and shudder. How could they have cut down vegetation for bedding? How could they have burnt wood? How could they have left their waste everywhere? It requires generational change for practices to become accepted and if we want our national parks to remain permanent public assets for our descendants, then some of these measures will be necessary.

Another possible scenario is the corporatisation, or even privatisation of our national parks. One can only imagine what effect an increasing emphasis on the user-pays principle will have on walking and camping; and what alterations big business might bring to national park administration in the name of maximising shareholder returns.

Stream Lily

10

Appendices

Appendix I: Gear checklist

ACCOMMODATION
Ground sheet
Pillowcase or pillow
Sleeping bag (+ liner
    if cold expected)
Sleeping mat
Tents (pegs/ropes)

CLOTHES
Boots (+ gaiters)
Wet-weather gear
    (Gore-Tex rain
    jacket and over-
    trousers if forecast
    particularly bad)
Dry night clothes
Sandals
Shorts (+ swimmers)
Socks
Thermals
T-shirts

HYGIENE
Comb
Earbuds
Deodorant
Insect repellent
Moisturiser

Razor
Soap/shampoo
Sunscreen
Tissues
Toilet paper
Toothbrush/
    toothpaste
Towel

ESSENTIALS
Underwear
Warm jumper
Warm slacks.

COOKING
Billy
Cup
Cutlery
Plates
Pots
Scouring pad
Spare fuel cartridge
Stove

MISCELLANEOUS
Candle
Compass
Repair kit

Gore-Tex bivvy if
    going solo
Cigarette lighter
Matches
Maps
Road maps
First aid kit
Pocket-knife/
    can-opener
Watch (altimeter)
Water bottles/
    container

CAR CAMPING
Extra changes of
    clothing
Games/activities
Methylated spirits or
    kerosene
Newspaper
Firelighters
Money
Pillow
Reading material
Table/chair set
Tool kit
Spare batteries
Water cannisters
Torch

Hat/cap
Weather forecast
Pen/paper
Plastic bags for
    garbage and
    waterproofing
Walker intention
    form
Resealable bags
    for food
Rope if required
Rubber bands
Salt if leeches
    expected
Sunglasses
Water filter if
    required

CAMERA
Bodies
Lenses
Tripod
Filter
Trigger release cable
Film
Camera bag
Spare battery
Case

Appendix II:

Walker intention form

Walk starts at:

Map   Grid ref:

On   day   date

At   hrs (time)

Vehicle registration nos:

Planned overnight camp locations:

Day 1 Map: Grid ref:

Day 2 Map: Grid ref:

Day 3 Map: Grid ref:

Day 4 Map: Grid ref:

Day 5 Map: Grid ref:

Day 6 Map: Grid ref:

Walk finishes at:

Map: Grid ref:

On   day   date

At   hrs (time)

Vehicle registration nos:

Group experience: experienced   novices

Walkers who have first aid certificates:

The group is carrying the following items:

Maps	Compasses	First aid kits
Extra food	Water	Warm clothing
Tents/shelter	Sleeping bags	Fire starters
Mirrors	Fuel stoves	Whistles
UHF CB radio	Mobile phone no	

Name

Name

Name

Name

Instructions

If the group has not returned or contacted you by:

    (time) on   (day)   (date)

Please contact:

Phone:

Appendix III: Mapping

For most of the popular walking areas of Australia, 1:25 000 topographical scale maps showing 10-metre contour intervals are available. Many alpine areas are covered at 1:50 000 scale, while more remote wilderness areas only have 20-metre intervals, which can be deceptive if you are used to reading features at a 10-metre resolution.

The best quality maps are those from Tasmania, because of recent surveying and printing using the latest technology. The colour schemes also provide information about the vegetation in the clearest manner. Note, however, that some negotiable routes in the Arthur Ranges are not included.

Coverage of New South Wales is the most complete, but unfortunately very out-of-date since most field revision was done in the 1970s. The Victorian maps are very good. Coverage of all national park regions has been completed recently with a reasonable level of detail.

Many parts of Western Australia and South Australia have yet to be covered because of the enormity of these states. The poorest quality and scantiest maps are of Queensland.

For those areas still neglected by state mapping departments, walkers might have to make do with the 1:100 000 AUSMAP series produced by the Commonwealth Government. This will require of walkers a minimum standard of navigational expertise and self-sufficiency.

Maps are generally available at most shops specialising in outdoor gear. Perhaps the best map shop in Australia is the Melbourne Map Centre, at 740 Waverley Road, Chadstone, Victoria, 3148. Their range includes virtually a complete coverage of government maps for all parts of the country and a vast number of other maps, including overseas.

Australian Capital Territory

The NSW Land Information Centre (LIC) also covers the complete Australian Capital Territory with their 1:25 000 scale, meeting bushwalkers' every need. Supplementary to this, the ACT Parks and Conservation Service has released a Namadgi National Park 1:100 000 map that includes information on adjoining state forests, wilderness areas and national parks in New South Wales.

New South Wales

The Land Information Centre (LIC) is the state government's official supplier of maps. The centre's address and postal map ordering department is:

LIC
Map sales counter
PO Box 143
Bathurst NSW 2795

There is also an office at 33 Bridge Street, Sydney.

The NSW LIC has agents all over the state where specific maps can be purchased; for example, camping stores, disposal stores, service stations, visitor centres, rangers' headquarters and information kiosks in national parks.

At present, the NSW LIC is working on producing a digital database of maps where new information can be updated immediately and user needs can be met more specifically. In the future, we should see new, updated editions of the state's topographical coverage.

In addition to their topographical coverage, the LIC has also released two series of tourist maps, with the emphasis on national parks and their environs. Called the Red Series and the Green Series, they are of a larger scale, often 1:100 000, and depict four-wheel-drive tracks, camping areas, picnic facilities, lookouts, watercourses, and so on.

Green series

Barrington Tops and Gloucester districts, including Chichester, Barrington Tops, Avon River, Stewarts Brook, Mount Royal, Masseys Creek, Bowman, Copeland Tops and Coneac State Forests

Kosciuszko National Park

Ku-ring-gai Chase National Park

Royal/Heathcote National Parks

Wollemi National Park, including Newnes, Lidsdale, Hampton, Nullo Mountain, Coricudgy, Putty, Comleroy and Kandos State Forests, Goulburn River National Park, Dharug National Park, Marramarra National Park, Cattai State Recreation Area, Pantoneys Crown Nature Reserve, Blue Mountains National Park (northern area) and Gardens of Stone National Park

Warrumbungle National Park

Red series

Albury/Wadonga

Armidale and districts, including New England, Oxley Wild Rivers, Guy Fawkes River National Park, Serpentine Nature Reserve, Styx River, Hyland, Nulla Five Day, Oakes, Clouds Creek, Ellis, Marengo, Thumb Creek, Mistake, Lower Creek, and Pee Dee State Forests

Batemans Bay/Ulladulla

Bathurst/Orange

Bega/Eden

Blue Mountains, including Kanangra Boyd National Park, Thirlmere Lakes National Park, Nattai National Park, Lake Burragorang, Bents Basin State Recreation Area, Norton Basin Reserve, Jenolan, Vulcan and Gurnang State Forests

Broken Hill/Menindee Lakes

Central Coast

Coffs Harbour

Dubbo/Wellington

Grafton

Hunter Valley

Inverell/Glen Innes

Kempsey

Lightning Ridge

Lismore

Mudgee

Murrumbidgee Irrigation Area

Port Macquarie

Port Stephens

Taree/Wingham

Tweed/Byron

Wagga Wagga

There is also a Waterways Series (Light Blue) with detailed coverage of the Myall Lakes, the Hawkesbury River, the Snowy Mountains lakes, Central Inland Lakes and Sydney Harbour.

The Dark Blue, a Regional Series of 11 broad-scaled regional maps gives an overview of a particular area: the New England Tablelands and adjoining coast, the Outback, the Murray Riverina, the Snowy Mountains and Canberra, the South Coast, the Hunter, the Golden West and Lord Howe Island.

The Forestry Commission of New South Wales produces a series of state forestry maps, which are not topographical but do show watercourses, reserves, roads, four-wheel-drive tracks, picnic facilities and camping areas. Coverage is confined to Tenterfield, Casino, Glen Innes, Coffs Harbour, Pilliga, Kempsey, Walcha, Port Macquarie, Barrington Tops, Bulahdelah, Newcastle, Bathurst, Nowra, Batemans Bay, Eden, Tumut and the Murray Valley.

Other types of maps include historical sketch-maps that are still useful today. They were drawn up by bushwalking pioneers such as Myles Dunphy in the Blue Mountains and the Budawang Committee members in the Morton National Park. These are available through larger camping stores such as Mountain Designs. They provide no topographical information but show negotiable routes: rough walking tracks that indicate passes through cliffs, on ridge tops, and camping spots by rivers in wild areas.

Queensland

SUNMAP produces the state's recreational mapping series. Because of the vast size of Queensland, only a fraction has been topographically mapped for walkers on a 1:25 000 series. Fortunately the best areas are covered—the Scenic Rim, and important wet tropical coastal range destinations. Specific national parks and popular destinations are the subject of a tourist map series that highlights attractions, picnic grounds, walks, and so on. There is also a complete 1:100 000 coverage. The maps can be obtained from the SUNMAP head office opposite the Gabba cricket ground at:

Corner Main and Vulture Streets
Woolloongabba Qld 4102

Agents are located all around the state. In addition, Adventure Maps publish maps of national parks, such as Lamington.

South Australia

The South Australian Department of Lands' Mapping Branch has produced a series of 1:50 000 topographical maps. These cover mainly the south-east of the state including the peninsulas, Adelaide, Kangaroo Island, Mount Gambier and surrounds, and the Flinders Ranges. Their primary outlet is:

Mapland
2 Pirie Street
Box 1047
Adelaide SA 5000

In addition, the South Australian Recreation Institute produces specialised walking maps of the Heysen Trail, Mount Lofty and more.

Tasmania

TASMAP produces the state series and is located in Hobart at 134 Macquarie Street. You can also order maps by mail from:

TASMAP
GPO Box 44A
Hobart Tas. 7001

The TASMAP sales office in Launceston is located at Henty House, 1 Civic Square.

The maps are widely sold in outdoor shops, bookshops and many newsagents. Most areas frequented by walkers are covered by the excellent 1:25 000 series with quality better than any other state in the country. Specific park maps at similarly useful scales are widely produced and available.

National parks maps	Day walk maps	
Asbestos Range	(1:25 000)	Ben Lomond
Ben Lomond	(1:50 000)	Cradle Mountain
Cradle Mountain	(1:100 000)	Hartz Mountains
Frenchmans Cap	(1:50 000)	Mount Roland
Freycinet	(1:50 000)	Mount Wellington
Douglas-Apsley	(1:50 000)	
Maria Island	(1:50 000)	
Mount Field	(1:50 000)	
Rocky Cape	(1:30 000)	
Walls of Jerusalem	(1:25 000)	

Unfortunately some of the far south-west region is not covered by 1:25 000 scale, but a set of 1:100 000 scale maps cover the entire state. There are two types of 1:100 000 maps: land tenures and pure topographicals.

Victoria

VICMAP, the state government's official supplier of maps, has its main outlet at:

318 Little Bourke Street
Melbourne Vic 3000

VICMAP has produced a series of recreational maps, collectively called the Outdoor Leisure Series. They contain detailed topographical lines and information notes on places of interest, walks and tourist facilities. Many have close-up and location maps. Some of these maps are at scales that can be useful to walkers.

Outdoor Leisure Series

East Gippsland	(1: 50 000)
Lake Tyers	(1: 25 000)
Bogong Alpine Area	(1: 50 000)
Buller–Stirling	(1: 25 000)
Lake Eildon	(1: 50 000)
Cathedral Range	(1: 25 000)
Marysville	(1: 30 000)
(Reverse: Lake Mountain)	(1: 10 000)
Kinglake National Park	(1: 25 000)
Wilsons Promontory National Park	(1: 50 000)
Otways and Shipwreck Coast	(1: 50 000)
Northern Grampians	(1: 50 000)
Southern Grampians	(1: 50 000)
Hattah Lakes	(1: 25 000)
Mallacoota (including Mallacoota Inlet)	(1: 50 000)

VICMAP's better series for walkers is the broad coverage of 1:25 000 sheets, but not all the state is covered by these. To the north-east the popular alpine and border regions, as well as East Gippsland, are covered by 1:50 000 scale. The maps are readily available throughout the state at outdoor gear shops, bookshops and at the Melbourne Map Centre in Chadstone.

Western Australia

A very limited 1:25 000 topographical coverage exists, especially of the national parks. A limited 1:50 000 coverage is applicable for some of the south-west region.

These areas are covered by tourist maps: Batavia Coast, Blackwood Valley, Gascoyne, Goldfields, the Greater South-West, the Kimberley, Pilbara, the Mid West, Rainbow Coast, Rottnest Island, South Coast, South-West Corner, and the Southern Forests.

They can be ordered through:
The Central Map Agency,
DOLA
Midland Square
Midland WA 6056

National

AUSMAP has produced an almost complete 1:100 000 topographical coverage of Australia. Contour intervals are generally 20 metres. They are printed in up to seven colours, including relief shading to give walkers a better visualisation of the landscape. However, like the state-based coverage, some of these maps are more than 10 years old, rendering them inadequate for areas such as state forests where new logging trails are being created all the time. AUSMAP also produces a series of national park tourist maps for Uluru, the Australian Alps and Kakadu. They all can be ordered through:
AUSLIG
PO Box 2
Belconnen ACT 2616

Other maps

For access to national parks, the states' various driver organisations (RACQ, RACV, NRMA, RACT, RAA) and petrol companies have statewide coverage of road maps. They augment this by including tourist maps of specific areas; for example, the Blue Mountains and the Southern Highlands.

Other useful maps originate from the *Australian Geographic* magazine, which cover specific natural areas such as East Gippsland and Lord Howe Island.

Appendix IV: Addresses of National Parks and Wildlife Services & environment agencies

Federal
Parks Australia–Wildlife Australia
GPO Box 636
Canberra ACT 2601
Phone: (02) 6250 0221

Australian Capital Territory
Environment Information Centre
Macarthur House
12 Wattle Street
(PO Box 144)
Lyneham ACT 2602
Phone: (02) 6207 9777

New South Wales
43 Bridge Street
(PO Box 1967)
Hurstville NSW 2220
Phone: 1300 36 1967 or (02) 9585 6333

Northern Territory
Darwin Region (Headquarters)
Goyder Centre
25 Chung Wah Terrace
(PO Box 496)
Palmerston NT 0831
Phone: (08) 89 995511

Queensland
Department of Environment
160 Ann Street
Brisbane Qld 4000
Phone: (07) 3227 8187

Tasmania
Parks and Wildlife Service
GPO Box 44A
Hobart Tas 7001
Phone: (03) 6233 6191

Victoria
Parks Victoria
Head Office
8 Nicholson Street
East Melbourne Vic 3002
Phone: (03) 9637 8000

Western Australia
Department of Land Administration
1 Midland Square
Midland WA 6056
Phone: (08) 9273 7373

Other useful addresses:
The Wilderness Society
130 Davey Street
Hobart Tas 7000
Phone: (03) 6234 9799

Australian Conservation Foundation
Head Office
340 Gore Street
Fitzroy Vic 3065
Phone: (03) 9416 1166 or 1800 332 510

Appendix V: Internet resources

The Internet is an outstanding source of up-to-date information on bushwalking and camping throughout Australia. The resources available on the following web pages include links to equipment manufacturers, online shopping for camping equipment, information about walking permits, the latest national park policy amendments, and more. The Newsgroup is a discussion forum for all interested walkers sharing current information and useful ideas.

Bushwalking and Camping Sites

Australian Bushwalking Web:
www.bushwalking.org.au

Australian Bushwalking &
Camping Reference Site:
www.galactic.net.au/bushwalking/mail.html

Tyrone T Thomas, author of *120 Walks of Victoria* and other state guidebooks:
www.ozemail.com.au/~tyronet

Australian National Parks:
www.atn.com.au/parks/index/html

David Noble's Bushwalking
and Canyoning site:
www.lisp.com.au/~daven/index.html

Yarrawood Bushwalking Club Inc:
www.ozemail.com.au/~yarrawd

The Wilderness Society:
www.wilderness.org.au

Australian Conservation Foundation:
www.acfonline.org.au

Wilderness Australia:
www.zeta.org.au/~avatar

Bogong On-Line Shopping:
www.bogong.com.au

Newsgroups

news:aus.bushwalking

Appendix VI: Addresses of camping stores

The following is a list of the best camping stores around the country. These retail chains are known for their quality brands and knowledgeable staff. Their prices are normally considerably more expensive than those of disposal stores, but their equipment will last longer and look after you better.

Australian Capital Territory
Kathmandu
20 Allara Street
Canberra City ACT 2601
Ph: (02) 6257 5926

Mountain Designs
6 Lonsdale Street
Braddon ACT 2612
Ph: (02) 6247 7488

Paddy Pallin
11 Lonsdale Street
Braddon ACT 2612
Ph: (02) 6257 3883

New South Wales
Kathmandu
Town Hall Arcade
Cnr Kent and Bathurst
    streets
Sydney NSW 2000
Ph: (02) 9261 8901

Mountain Designs
499 Kent Street
Sydney NSW 2000
Ph: (02) 9267 3822

Paddy Pallin
507 Kent Street
Sydney NSW 2000
Ph: (02) 9264 2685

Queensland
Kathmandu
144 Wickham Street
Fortitude Valley Qld 4006
Ph: (07) 3252 8054

Mountain Designs
105 Albert Street
Brisbane Qld 4000
Ph: (07) 3221 6756

Paddy Pallin
138 Wickham Street
Fortitude Valley Qld 4006
Ph: (07) 3252 4408

South Australia
Mountain Designs
203 Rundle Street
Adelaide SA 5000
Ph: (08) 8232 0690

Paddy Pallin
228 Rundle Street
Adelaide SA 5000
Ph: (08) 8232 3155

Tasmania
Mountain Designs
74 Elizabeth Street
Hobart Tas 7000
Ph: (03) 6234 3900

Paddy Pallin
76 Elizabeth Street
Hobart Tas 7000
Ph: (03) 6231 0777

Victoria
Kathmandu
372 Little Bourke Street
Melbourne Vic 3000
Ph: (03) 9642 1942

Mountain Designs
377 Little Bourke Street
Melbourne Vic 3000
Ph: (03) 9670 3354

Paddy Pallin
360 Little Bourke Street
Melbourne Vic 3000
Ph: (03) 9670 4845

Western Australia
Mountain Designs
862 Hay Street
Perth WA 6000
Ph: (08) 9322 4774

Appendix VII: Key to reserve classifications

National Park–The definition of the International Union for the Conservation of Nature and Natural Resources (UCN) in classifying a national park is:

> ... a relatively large area where one or several ecosystems are not materially altered by human exploitation and occupation...and where visitors are allowed to enter under special conditions, for inspiration, education, cultural, and recreative purposes.

Another, simpler, definition is:

> ... an extensive area of public land of nationwide significance because of its outstanding natural features and diverse land types, set aside to provide public enjoyment, education, and inspiration in natural environments.

These reserves have high conservation, scenic and recreational values, and are usually larger than 4000 hectares. Despite the prefix 'national', they are state-managed. The special conditions referred to include the prohibition of pets, firearms, and cutting equipment, seasonal fire bans, and the requirement of vehicle registration. Rangers have the authority to evict people and impose penalties on those who do not observe the regulations.

State Recreation Area (SRA)–A State Recreation Area is a smaller reserve than a national park that often protects only a particular feature, rather than a self-sustained ecosystem. These are part of the reserve system in New South Wales and are similar in tenure to Victoria's state parks. Regulations are less restrictive than in national parks, with the emphasis being more towards public recreation rather than conservation. One of the most popular State Recreation Areas is Bungonia near Goulburn.

Nature Reserve–This type of reserve is the highest level of protection that can be awarded in the state. Usually a particular type of rare environment is preserved: for example, coastal rainforest in Broken Head Nature Reserve. Facilities are very limited–in many, camping is prohibited altogether. One of the suggested walks in this guide is through the Pantoneys Crown Nature Reserve in the Capertee Valley, New South Wales.

State Forest– State Forests are managed by the Forestry Commission of New South Wales for the purpose of timber production, which generates about $100 million income. The forests can either take the form of softwood radiata pine plantations or native eucalypt hardwoods. There are just over 3.5 million hectares of state forest in New South Wales, 95 per cent of which is native. Recreation activities are well-catered-for in state forests–roads are generally widespread and of better quality than in national parks. Picnic and camping areas are abundant in popular regions, and restrictions are usually minimal. While the scenery is generally not as beautiful as in national parks, the sheer scale and relative ease of access of state forests make them ideal for extended exploration.

Flora, Fauna, Forest Reserves–These small reserves, often found along tourist drives in state forests and with picnic and camping facilities, preserve particularly sensitive or attractive areas for conservation and recreational purposes. Primarily, they act as a reference point against which to judge the effects of logging elsewhere. Despite popular belief, these reserves have full legislation-backed protection, and can only be revoked by parliament.

Catchment Authority/Water Board Territory–After the contamination debacle with Sydney's drinking water in 1998, there is now a far greater emphasis on maintaining the purity of urban water supply catchment areas. The states' various water utilities jointly administer large proportions of the natural land surrounding state capitals. In the Blue Mountains, the construction of Warragamba Dam in 1960 blocked the Coxs and Wollondilly River valleys, forming a massive stored water build-up known as Lake Burragorang. A three-kilometre circumference around this 7500-hectare lake is totally prohibited to bushwalkers and campers.

Other water authorities' regulations are more relaxed, such as the Tasmanian Hydro-Electric Commission, with canoeing and power boating permitted on stored water.

World Heritage Area–These are areas of outstanding natural and/or cultural significance registered with UNESCO in Paris. Australia has Kinchega National Park as its first World Heritage Area, although Uluru and the Great Barrier Reef would be our most famous areas. Tasmania has 20 per cent of its area–equivalent to 1.38 million hectares–classified as world heritage. Land tenure is determined by state legislation, but international agreements and Commonwealth legislation regulate management frameworks. A related reservation status is the UNESCO Biosphere Reserve, which acts as a control against which human impact on pristine areas is monitored and recorded. Kosciuszko National Park in New South Wales is an example of this type of reserve.

State Reserve–These are generally less than 4000 hectares in size, and preserve a particular feature or site. An example is Hastings Caves in Tasmania.

Game Reserve–These areas, such as Bruny Island Neck, Tasmania, offer the same level of protection as state reserves, but allow for certain species to be hunted by permit.

Conservation Area–Such areas provides protection from the actions of the public, but not from actions undertaken in pursuance of a right granted under other legislation. The level of protection of a conservation area can be expanded by the implementation of a statutory management plan of the area. Examples are the Central Plateau and Cape Direction in Tasmania.

Protected Areas–These enjoy a similar degree of protection to conservation areas, allowing a controlled use of resources but reserved under the Crown Lands Act (Tasmania) 1976. An example is Mount Roland in northern Tasmania.

State Park–These are generally smaller than 4000 hectares and preserve a particular feature or site, such as Lake Eildon in Victoria. Recreational facilities are more common, but are managed on the same principles as national parks.

Coastal Park/Marine Reserve–Because of the popularity of water, these reserves and Lakeside Reserves are managed on a multi-utilitarian basis where the aquatic and marine natural environment is protected and access and facilities are provided for public enjoyment. About 90 per cent of Victoria's 2000-kilometre coastline is publicly owned, of which two-thirds is managed by Parks Victoria in over 300 reserves totalling 47 000 hectares. An example is the Phillip Island Penguin Reserve.

Historic Site–This can be a prehistoric, historic or cultural feature on public land managed by the department within national, state, regional and coastal parks as well as state forests.

Other–These include bushland reserves; flora and fauna reserves, such as Wychitella; in Victoria, flora reserves; historic parks, such as Pirianda Garden, also in Victoria; public purpose reserves; scenic lookout reserves; wilderness areas; and crown land.

Appendix VIII: Further reading

GENERAL READING

Alcorta, Frank. 1997, *Explore Australia's Northern Territory*, New Holland.

Andrews, Bill. 1997, *Explore Australia's Great Inland*, New Holland.

Australian Alps Liaison Committee. 1998, *Explore the Australian Alps*, New Holland.

Axcell, Claudia; Cooke, Diana; and Kimmount, Vikki. 1986, *Simple Foods for the Pack: The Sierra Club Guide to Delicious Natural Foods for the Trail*, Sierra Club Books.

Baxter, Nick. 1992, *Getting Started*, Wild Publications.

Carter, Simon. 1998, *Rock Climbing in Australia*, New Holland.

Colls, Keith and Whitaker, Richard. 1996, *The Australian Weather Book*, New Holland.

Goll, J. 1992, *The Camper's Pocket Handbook: A Backcountry Traveller's Companion*, ICS Books.

Hartung, E.J., Malin, D. and Frew, D.J., *Hartung's Astronomical Objects for Southern Telescopes: A Handbook for Amateur Observers*, Cambridge.

Hodgson, M. 1992, *Camping for Mere Mortals: It Ain't No Five Star Hotel*, ICS Books.

Jacobson, C. 1987, *Camping Secrets: A Lexicon of Camping Tips Only the Experts Know*, ICS Books.

Land Information Centre. 1984, *CMA Map Reading Guide*, Land Information Centre.

Mirtschin, Peter and Davis, Richard. 1992, *Snakes of Australia - Dangerous and Harmless*, Hill of Content.

Paddy Pallin. 1995, *Bushwalking and Camping*, Paddy Pallin.

Ridpath, I. 1990, *The Pocket Guide to Astronomy*, Parkgate Books.

Swan, Gerry. 1996, *A Photographic Guide to Snakes and Other Reptiles of Australia*, New Holland.

Swan, Gerry. 1998, *Snakes and Other Reptiles of Australia*, Green Guide Series, New Holland.

Toghill, Jeff. 1997, *Knots and Splices*, New Holland.

Wilson, Sally. 1997, *Some Plants are Poisonous*, New Holland.

GUIDEBOOKS

Queensland

Buchanan, Ross. 1996, *Bushwalking in South-East Queensland*, Hema Maps.

Buchanan, Ross and Buchanan, Heather. 1996, *Fraser Island and Cooloola Visitors Guide*, Hema Maps.

Jarrott, Keith L. 1990, *History of Lamington National Park*, J.K. Jarrott and the National Parks Association of Queensland.

Sinclair, John (with Peter Corris). 1994, *Fighting for Fraser Island*, Kerr Publishing.

Thomas, Tyrone. 2000, *50 Walks in North Queensland*, Hill of Content.

New South Wales

Budawang Committee. 1988, *Fitzroy Falls and Beyond*, Budawang Committee.

Budawang Committee. 1982, *Pigeon House and Beyond*, Budawang Committee.

Cameron, Bruce. 1992, *A History of the Blue Labyrinth*, Blue Mountains National Park, self-published..

Chapman, John. 1997, *Classic New South Wales Walks*, Wild Publications.

Doughton, Ron. 1989, *Bushwalking in the Budawangs*, Envirobook.

Dunk, Anthony. 1999, *Discovering the Colo Wilderness on Foot*, Envirobook.

Higgins, Les and Rodd, Tony. 2000. *A Day In the Bush: Sydney Region Bushwalks*, New Holland.

Hill, Harry. 1993, *Hume and Hovell Walking Track Guidebook.*

Klinge, Sven. 1994, *Cycling the Bush, 100 Rides in NSW*, Hill of Content.

McDougall, Garry and Shearer-Heriot, Leigh. 1998, *The Great North Walk*, Kangaroo Press.

National Parks Association. 1997, *Volume 1, Bushwalks in the Sydney Region*, NPA.

National Parks Association. 1998, *Volume 2, Bushwalks in the Sydney Region*, NPA.

Noble, David. 1996, *Blue Mountains Canyons*, Wild Publications.

Noble, David. 1996, *Classic Blue Mountains Walks*, Wild Publications.

Paton, Neil. 1986, *Sydney Bushwalks*, Kangaroo Press.

Paton, Neil. 1986, *Treks in New South Wales*, Kangaroo Press.

Paton, Neil. 1987, *Walks in the Blue Mountains*, Kangaroo Press.

Prineas, Peter and Gold, Henry. 1997, *Wild Places, Wilderness in Eastern New South Wales*, Colong Foundation.

Siseman, John. 1998, *Alpine Walking Track*, Pindari Publications.

Sloss, Robert William. 1992, *Mittagong Nattai - Walking Tracks for the Southern Highlands*, self-published.

Thomas, Tyrone. 1999, *120 Walks in New South Wales*, Hill of Content.

Thomas, Tyrone. 1998, *70 Walks in Southern New South Wales*, Hill of Content.

Thomas, Tyrone. 1998, *70 Walks in Southern New South Wales and A.C.T.*, Hill of Content.

UNE Mountaineering Club. 1984, *A Guide to North-Eastern New South Wales*, UNE Mountaineering Club.

Warner, Charles. 1989, *Bushwalking in Kosciuszko National Park.*

Williams, Bruce. 2000. *Blue Mountains on Foot*, New Holland.

ACT Parks and Conservation Service. 1999, *Namadgi National Park Map and Guide*, Environment ACT.

Victoria

Cook, Peter and Dowd, Chris. 1996, *Walking the Wilderness Coast*, Wildcoast Publications.

Chapman, John. 1999, *Classic Victorian Alpine Walks*, Wild Publications.

Da Costa, Grant. 1998, *Car Touring and Bushwalking in East Gippsland*, Australian Conservation Foundation.

Friends of the Great South West Walk. (Editor - Bennett, Gwen) 1996, *A Walk on the Wildside - The Great South-West Walk*, Friends of the Great South West Walk.

Geelong Bushwalking Club. 1996, *Walking the Otways*, Geelong Bushwalking Club.

Klinge, Sven. 1994, *Cycling the Bush, 100 Rides in Victoria*, Hill of Content.

Siseman, John. 1997, *Victoria's Alpine National Park*, Macstyle Media.

Thomas, Tyrone. 2000, *120 Walks in Victoria*, Hill of Content.

Thomas, Tyrone. 1991, *50 Walks in the Grampians*, Hill of Content.

Thomas, Tyrone. 2000, *60 Walks in Central Victoria's Gold Fields and Spa Country*, Hill of Content.

Thomas, Tyrone. 2000, *70 Walks in Victoria's Bright and Falls Creek Districts*, Hill of Content.

van de Knijff, Glen. 1992, *Extended Walks in the Victorian Alps*, Wild Publications.

Tasmania

Brand, Ian. 1984, *Sarah Island - An Account of the penal settlements of Sarah Island, Tasmania, from 1822 to 1833 and 1846 to 1847*, Regal Publications.

Chapman, John. 1998, *Cradle Mountain - Lake St Clair and Walls of Jerusalem National Park*, John Chapman and Pindari Publications.

Chapman, John. 1998, *South West Tasmania*, J. Chapman.

Chapman, John. 1994, *Wild Alternative Tasmania*, Wild Publications.

Collins, Ken. 1990, *South-West Tasmania*, Heritage Books.

Klinge, Sven. 1993, *Cycling the Bush: 100 Rides in Tasmania*, Hill of Content.

Siseman, John and Chapman, John. *Cradle Mountain - Lake St Clair National Park*

Storey, Peter and Storey, Shirley. 1996, *Tasman Tracks*, Koonya Press.

Thomas, Tyrone. 2000, *100 Walks in Tasmania*, Hill of Content.

South Australia

Bird, Peter and Fisher, David. 1995, *Walks with Nature – 20 Nature Walks in the Mount Lofty Ranges*, Nature Conservation Society of South Australia.

Conservation Council of South Australia. 1997, *Flinders Ranges Walks*, Federation of South Australian Walking Clubs.

Heard, Adrian. 1990, *Gammon Ranges and Arkaroola Sanctuary: A Walking Guide to the Northern Flinders Ranges*, State Publishing.

Barker, Sue (Editor). 1995, *Explore the Flinders Ranges*, Royal Geographical Society of Australasia (SA Branch).

Western Australia

Department of Conservation and Land Management (CALM). 1998, *A Guide to the Bibbulmum Track, Northern Half*, CALM.

Department of Conservation and Land Management (CALM). 1998, *A Guide to the Bibbulmum Track, Southern Half*, CALM.

Department of Conservation and Land Management (CALM). 1997, *Bushwalks in the South-West*, CALM.

Department of Conservation and Land Management (CALM). 1996, *Family Walks in the Perth Outdoors*, CALM.

Department of Conservation and Land Management (CALM). 1997, *More Family Walks in the Perth Outdoors*, CALM.

Morphet, A. T. 1996, *Mountain Walks in the Stirling Range, A pictorial guide: Part 1: The peaks to the west of Chester Pass*, Torridon Publications.

Morphet, A. T. 1996, *Mountain Walks in the Stirling Range, A pictorial guide: Part 2: The peaks to the west of Chester Pass*, Torridon Publications.

Conservation Commission of NT. 1995, *Explore Australia's Northern Territory*, Conservation Commission of NT.

Australia-wide

Chapman, John and Chapman, Monica. 1997, *Bushwalking in Australia*, Lonely Planet.

Chapman, John. 1991, *Gorge Walks*, Wild Publications.

Chapman, John. 1994, *Wild Peak Bagging*, Wild Publications.

Chapman, John. 1992, *Wild Waterfalls*, Wild Publications.

Dunphy, Myles. 1986, *Myles Dunphy – Selected Writings* (annotated by Patrick Thompson), Ballagirin.

Hermes, Neil. 1997, *Explore Wilderness Australia*, New Holland.

Klinge, Sven. 2000, *Classic Walks of Australia*, New Holland.

Klinge, Sven. 1996, *Cycling the Bush: The Best Rides in Australia*, Hill of Content.

Meredith, Peter. 1999, *Myles and Milo*, Allen & Unwin.

Rankin, Robert. 1996, *Classic Wild Walks of Australia*, Rankin (also available on CD-ROM) .

Thomas, Tyrone. 2000, *20 Best Walks in Australia*, Hill of Content.

Thomas, Tyrone and Klinge, Sven. 1998, *Australian Mountains: The Best 100 Walks*, Hill of Content.

Index